Old Cambuslang
at the turn of the century

Doreen Shepherd

Best wishes
Doreen Shepherd

Acknowledgements

The history of Cambuslang has been documented in many books and I have drawn valuable information from the following sources:-
A History of Cambuslang by James Alexander Wilson, OBE, MD; *The Old, New and Third Statistical Accounts of Lanarkshire (Cambuslang Section); Old Cambuslang, More Old Cambuslang, Around Old Cambuslang* and *Cambuslang in Old Picture Postcards* by Ian L Cormack, MA; *At the Sign of the Fish* by the Reverend Ian P. Davidson, MA.

I gratefully acknowlege permission to use their material granted by the following:-

Scott Crichton who contributed the most (glass slides 1-7, 12-18, 20-27, 29-32, 35 and 37-41; postcards 19, 28 and 47)
Mrs Eleanor Jones Griffiths (9, 10)
Miss Jane Harvie (11)
Jack Hastie (33, 34, 36)
Author (postcards 42-46)

I thank John Francis Quinn for his representation of 'Hallside Public School 1882', and Brian Lochrin for photography. Mention must be made of help given by J Neil Baxter, Grant Wilson, John Scoular, Denis Carpy, JS Johnstone and Brian Deans, BA, MSc. Thanks are due to Harry Dunlop, Rutherglen Museum; the staff of the Glasgow Room, Mitchell Library; Cambuslang Library and Halfway Library; Susie Stirling, Museum of Transport; *Rutherglen Reformer and Cambuslang Journal.* Special thanks to my son Gordon Shepherd for his support.

Introduction

There are always pictures of interest stored away in cupboards and attics and I have decided to produce more in *'Old Cambuslang—at the turn of the century'*. Many of the photographers of the 19th century produced beautiful and fascinating work. Examples from the 1890's have been produced here from the original glass slides. At this time there was a great rise in the sale of photographs and, later, postcards to tourists and collectors.

Every effort has been made to check for inaccuracies and I crave forgiveness for any unintentional mistakes.

The book is dedicated to the memory of the late Tom Crichton.

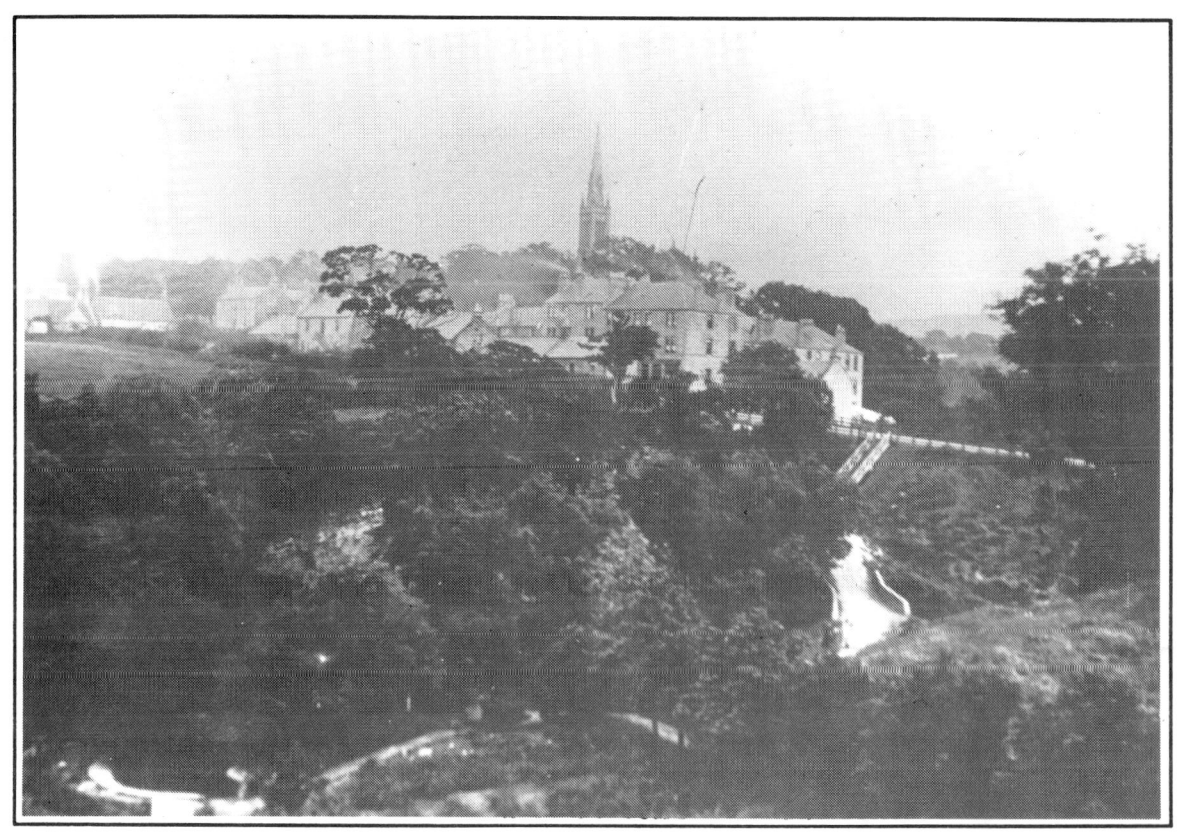

1. A view of Kirkhill in the 1890's shows the Borgie Glen and the old Kirkhill Brae (now Vicarland Road) leading to the Old Parish Church, with its fine spire and arches, which opened 1841. The tenement building known as the Rookery was densely populated with people, as were the trees with rooks!

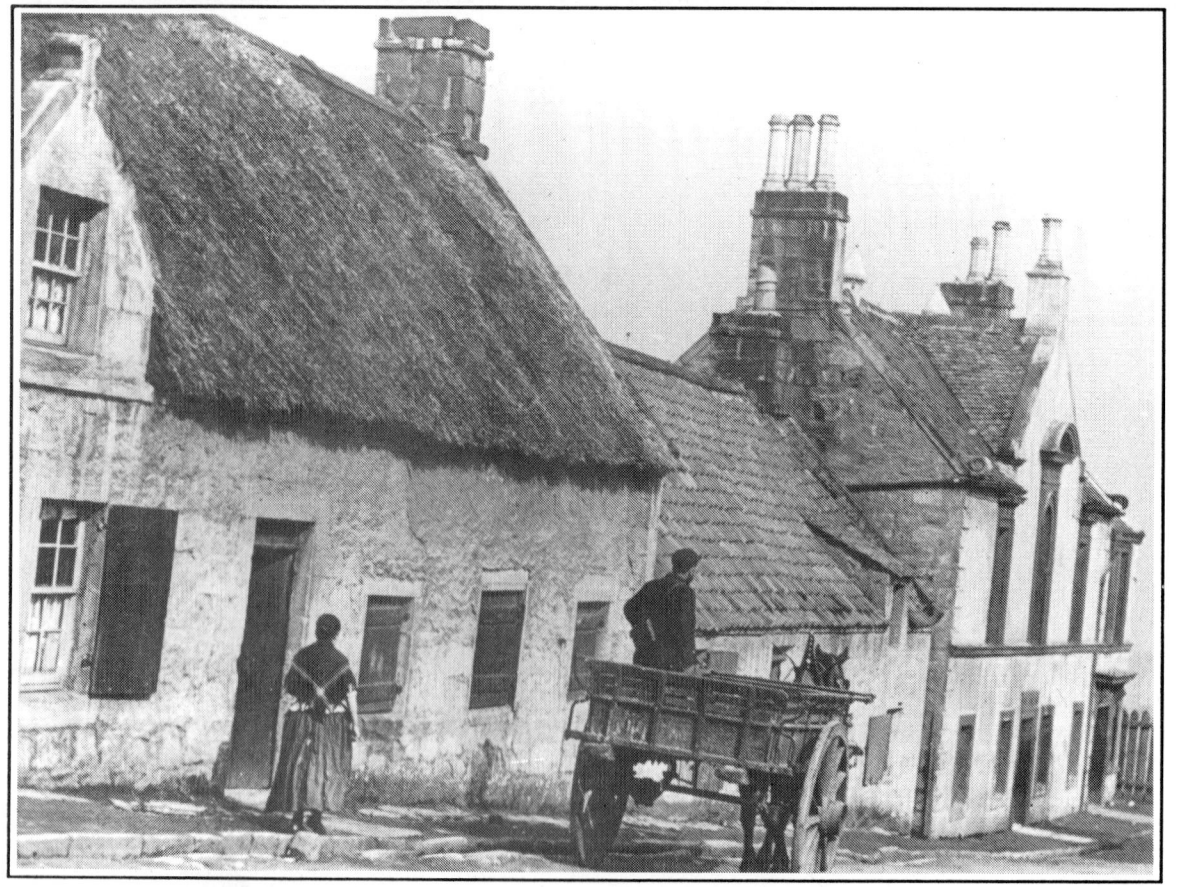

2. These old houses, as seen in the 1890's, were situated in Cadoc Street, Kirkhill named after the 'Patron Saint' of Cambuslang. The last building is the old Masonic Hall. Note the woman's style of dress including the shawl and the moneybag slung over the driver's shoulder. His street cry may have been, "Rags, bones, bottles or brass. Any old trousers without the ......!"

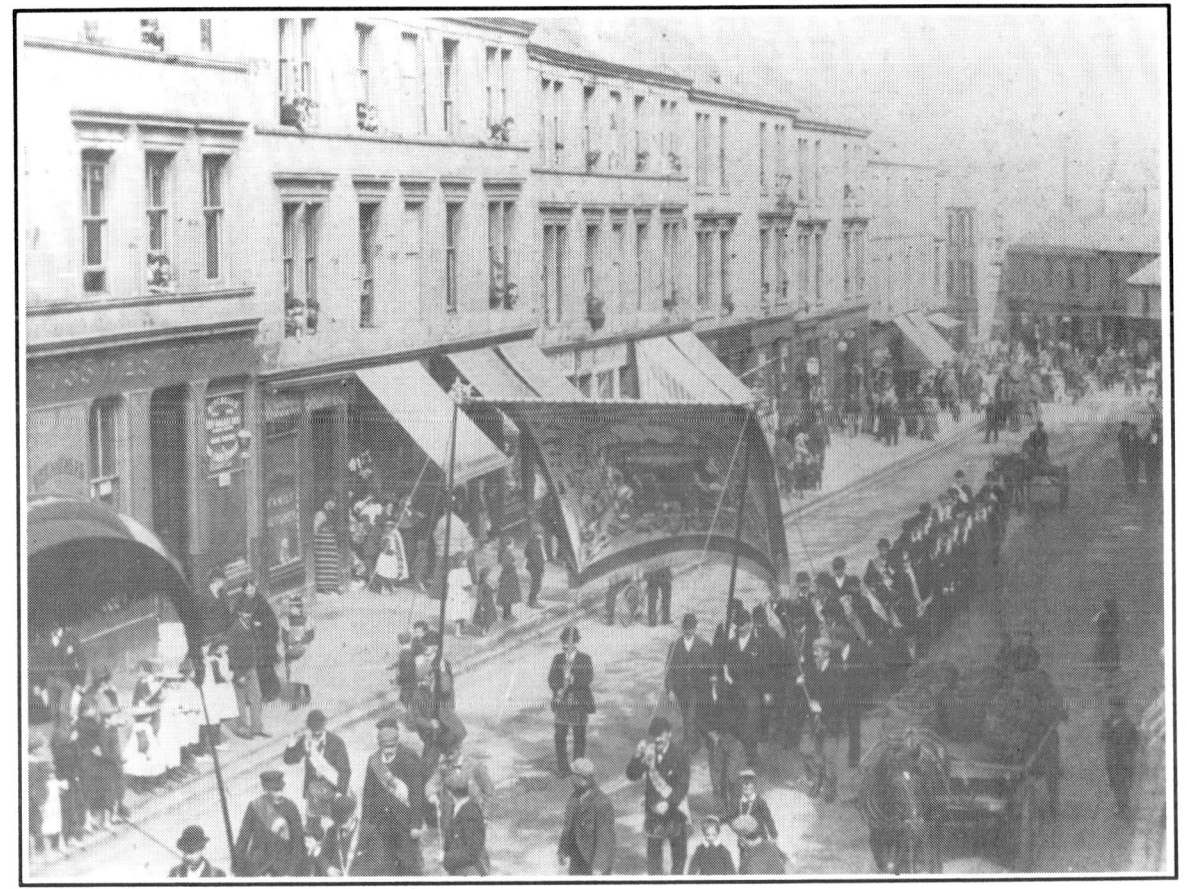

3. The parade of the Shepherds Friendly Society Limited is pictured in the 1890's passing along the Main Street, Cambuslang. The first objects of the Society were to provide some form of burial and sickness insurance, long before the State Acts were passed. Spectators, many with bare feet, are supporting the 'Working Man's Insurance Cover'.

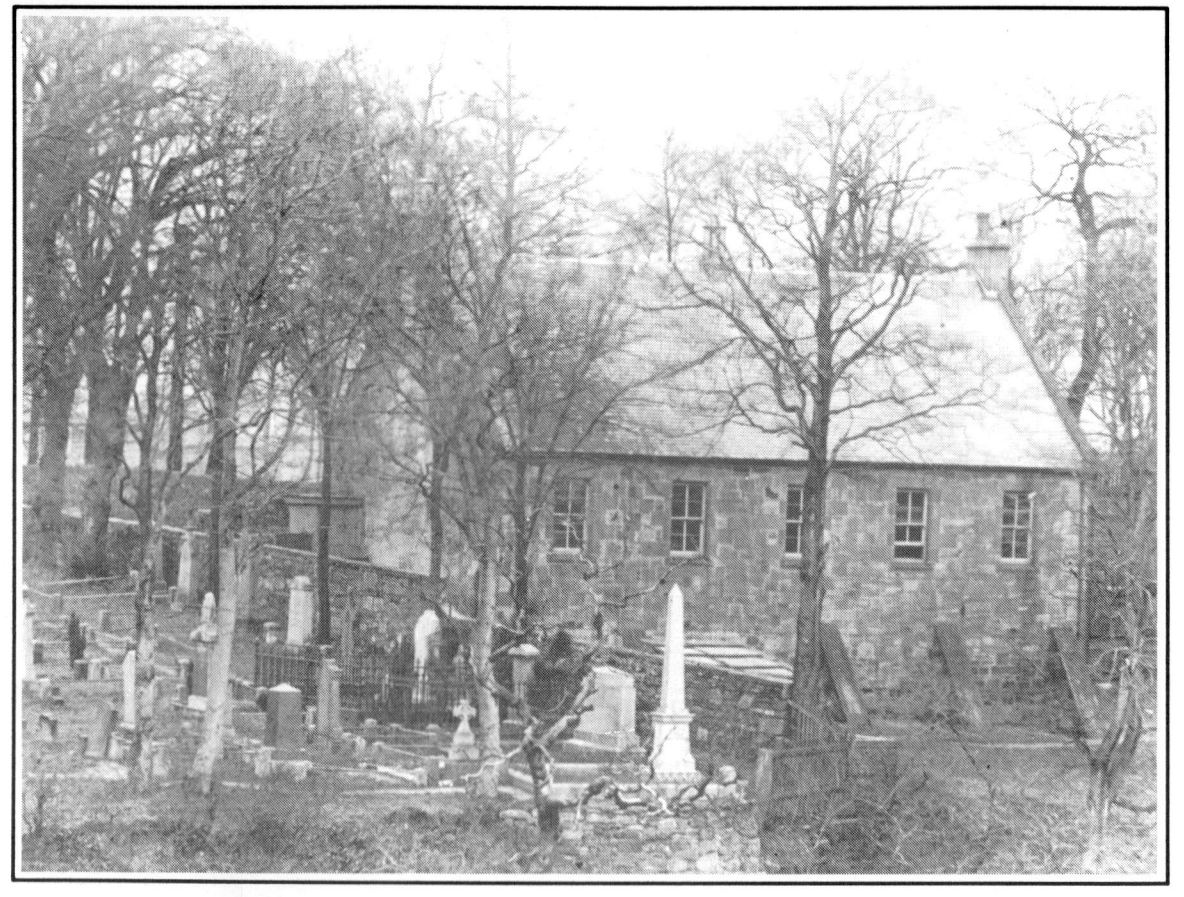

4. The present Halls of Cambuslang Old Parish Church seen at the turn of the century. They cost £1,818 to build and were opened in 1897 and refurbished and extended in 1968.

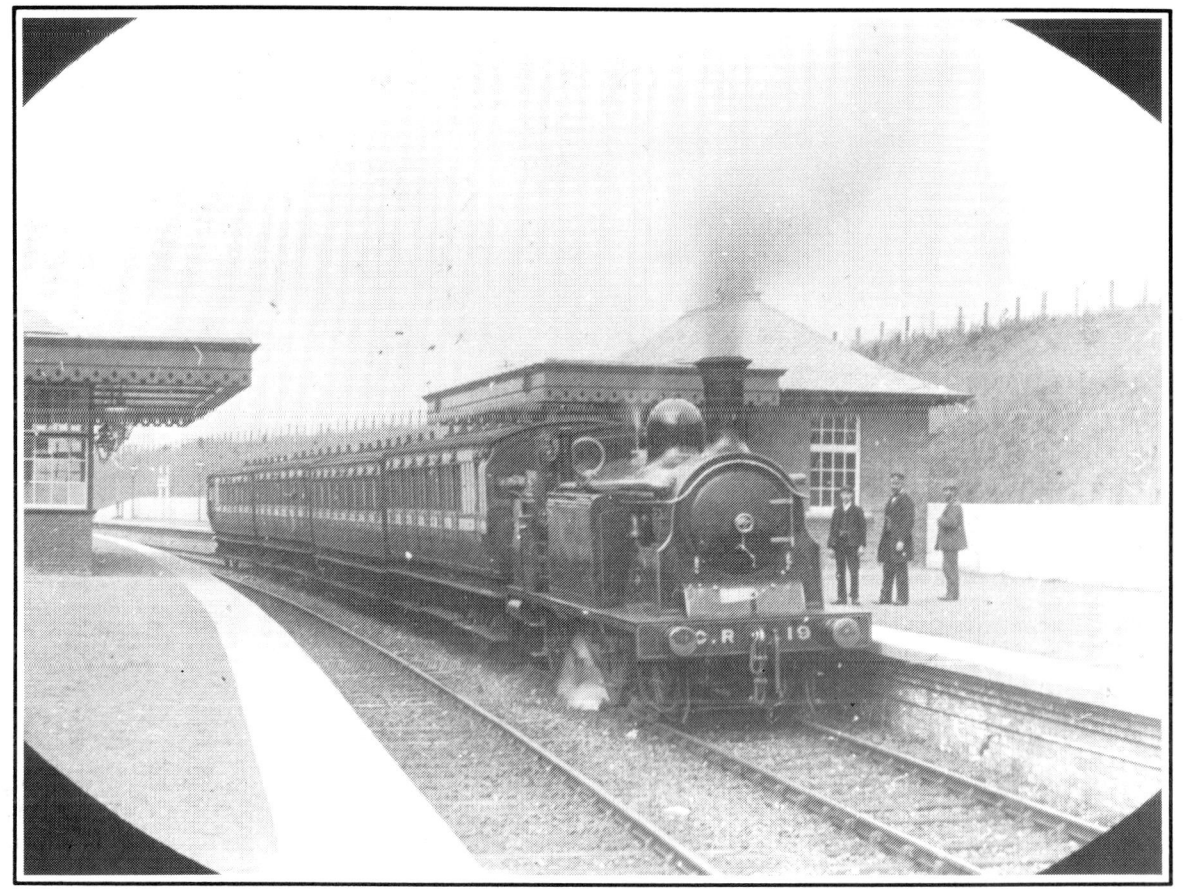

5. Kirkhill Station was opened on 6 January 1904. This view c 1906 shows the Caledonian Railway locomotive No 19 pulling a crowded train. In attendance were the stationmaster and a porter.

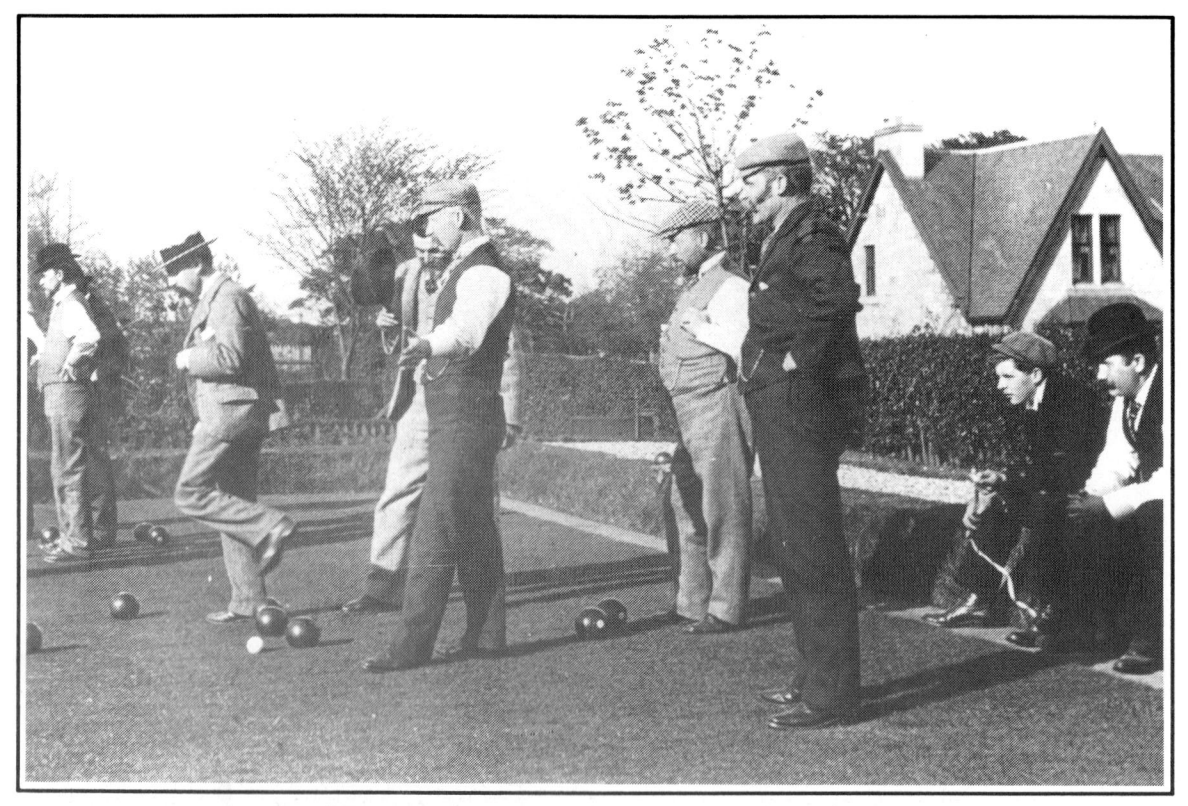

6. A group of Cambuslang bowlers 'looking for the shot'. Cambuslang Bowling Club was instituted in 1874 by shareholders, and in 1878 is referred to as Cambuslang/Wellshot Bowling Club. The name of the first president of the Ladies' Section, Mrs Hastie, appears on the Presidents' Board in 1924.

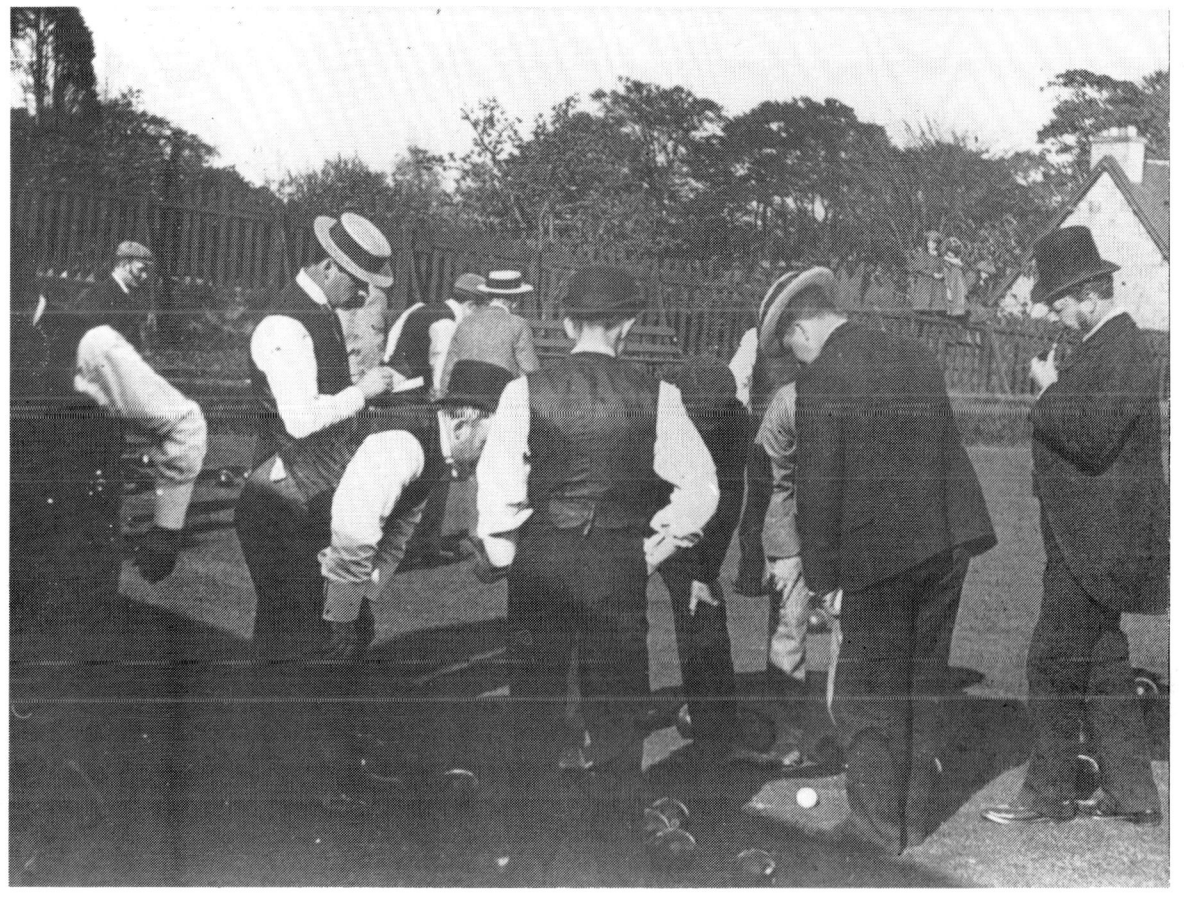

7. A close end for bowlers of Cambuslang Bowling Club in the 1890's. As well as gold cups and medals, the prizes in those days included three tons of coal, ten pounds of tea, a leg of mutton and barrels of apples!

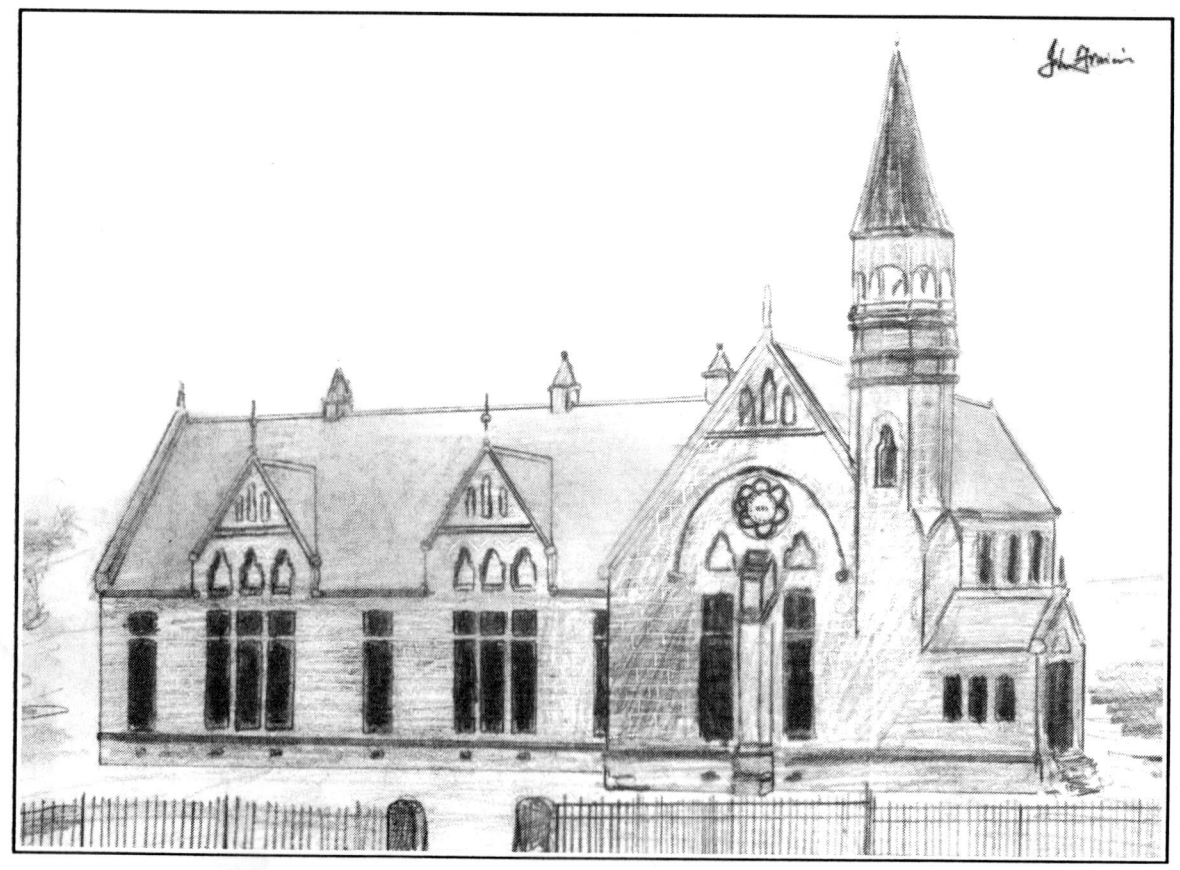

8. Artist's representation of Hallside Public School in 1882. The architect was Mr A Lindsay Miller. It is built in the Gothic style with decorative mouldings. The tripartate windows were highly regarded and can be seen headed by a trefoil tympanum. The little entrance offset is given emphasis by the low bell-tower. There are now three extensions and three hutted classrooms added. The school is due for closure in 1995, after 113 years, to make way for the new school being built.

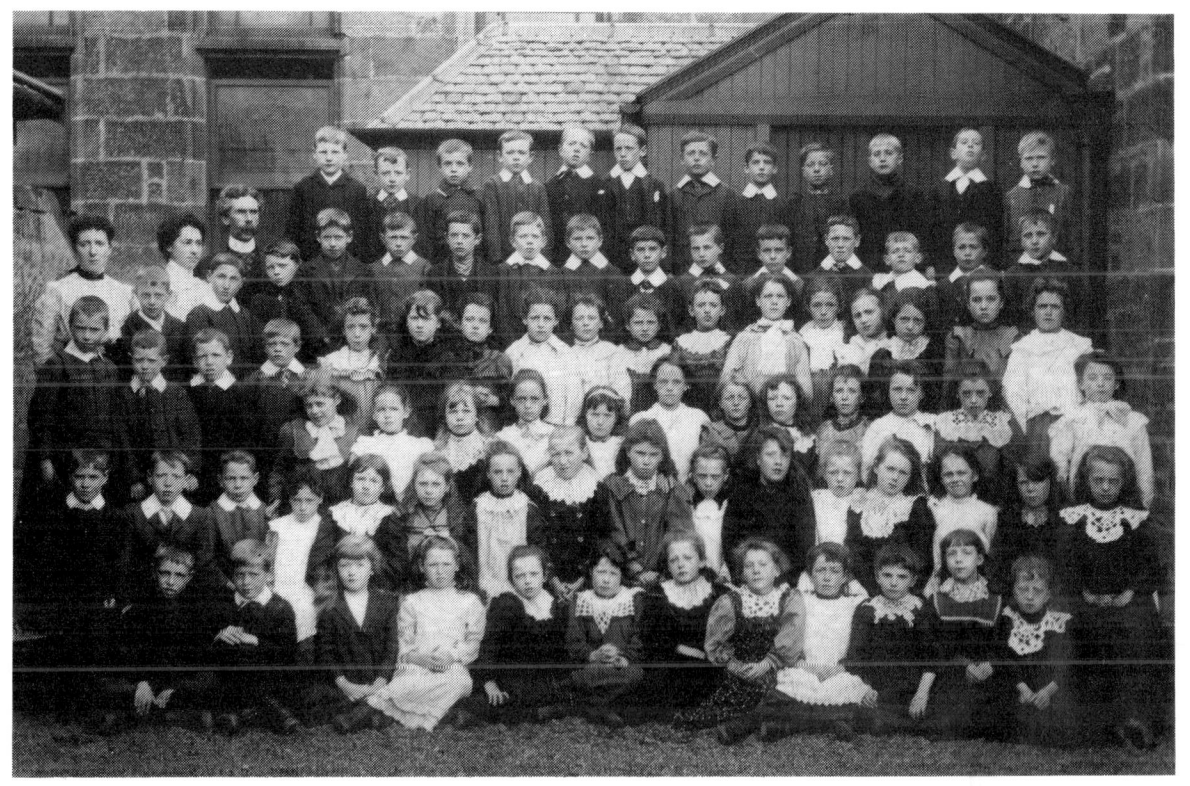

9. "That's me with my hair cut short. They did that to me when I got the measles" (Eleanor Jones b1889). Here they are, the Hallside Public School children c 1901. Boys have scrubbed rubber collars, there are no bare feet in sight and it is a serious occasion. The back row have "heads up" thanks to the training of Sgt Reid (Janitor) who gave military drill.

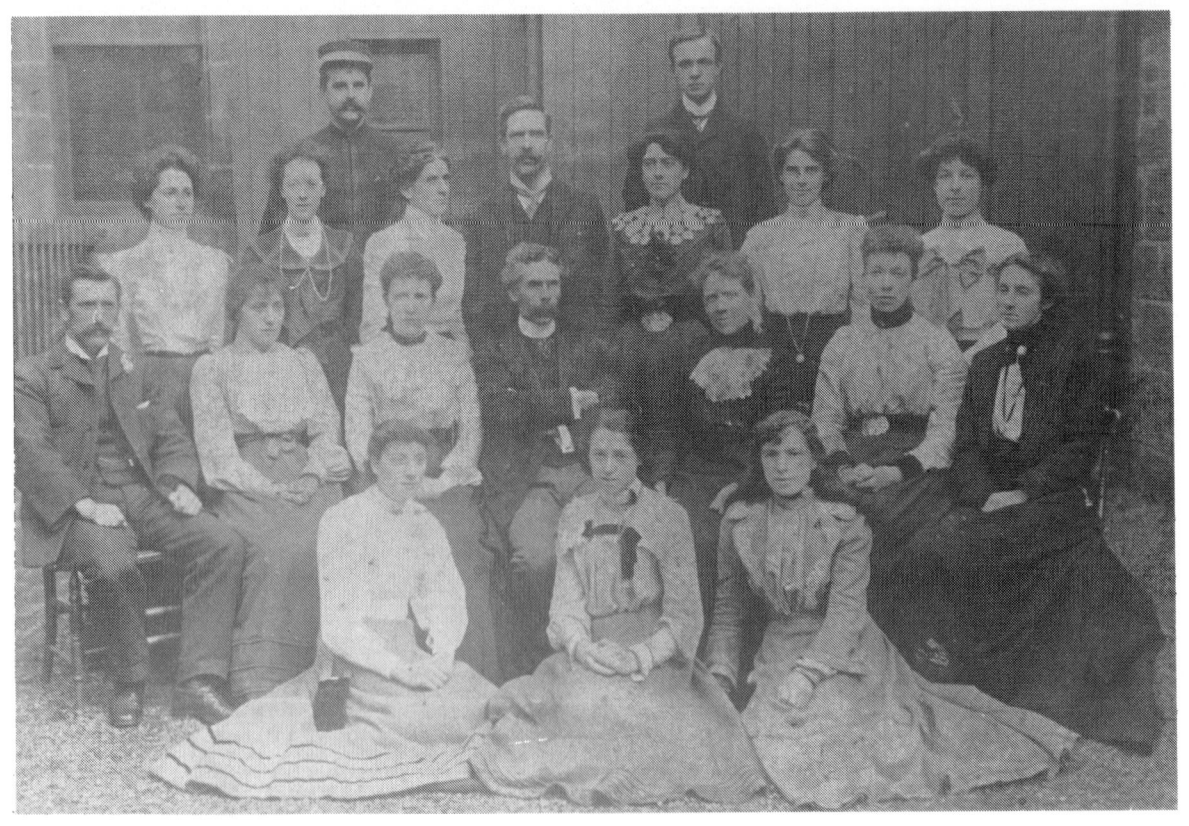

10. The staff of Hallside Public School c 1901 were Headmaster: A Brown; Headmistress: I Brisbane; Certificated Assistants: J Buchanan, A Aitken, E Macfarlane, G Macfarlane, K Semple, H Somerville, A House, A Anderson LLA, M Arrol; Assistants under Articles 60 and 79: M MacIntyre, J Fraser, M O Brown; Pupil teacher: A Purse; Monitor: W Simmons. The janitor is Sgt A Reid.

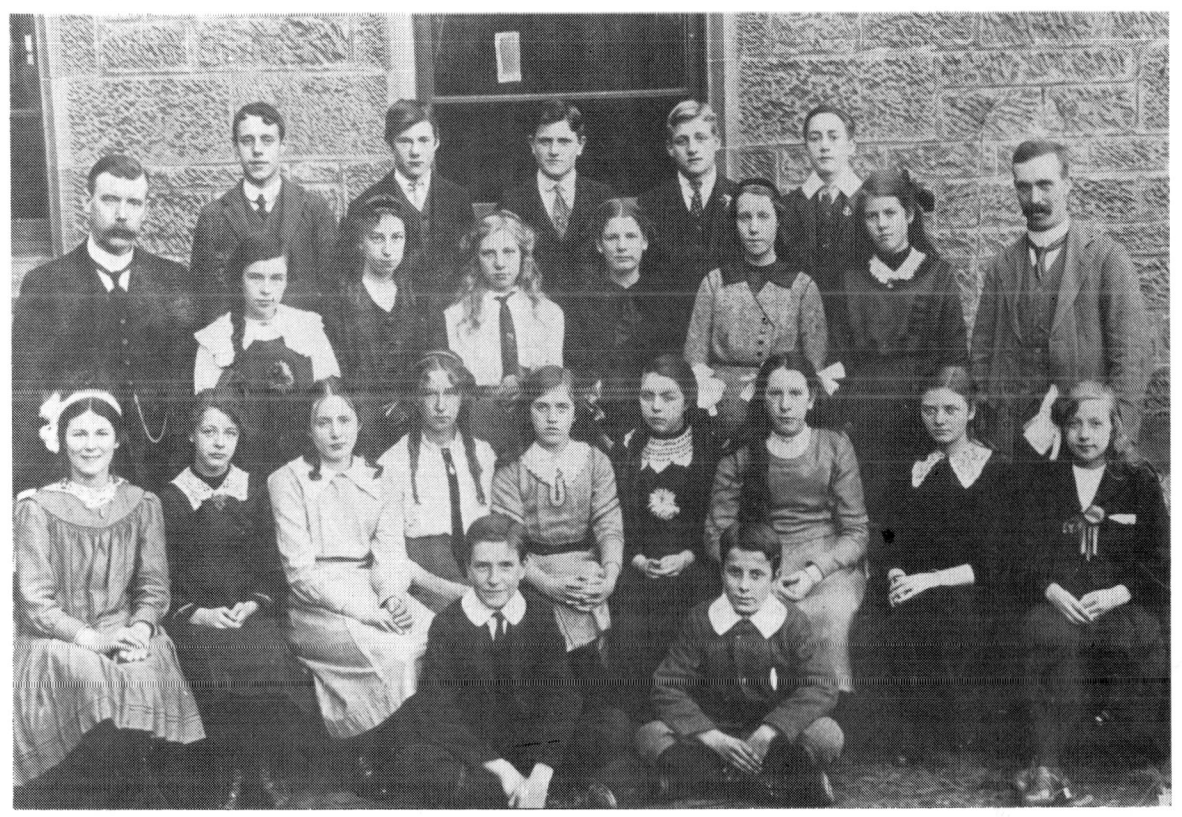

11. Class of West Coats Higher Grade School in 1911. The Higher Grade was added in 1910 for free, advanced classes and the chance to gain a group leaving certificate. The staff are Mr Mair and Mr Stewart. Jane Harvie (first girl, centre row) received silver and gold medals for perfect attendances at both Hallside and West Coats Schools.

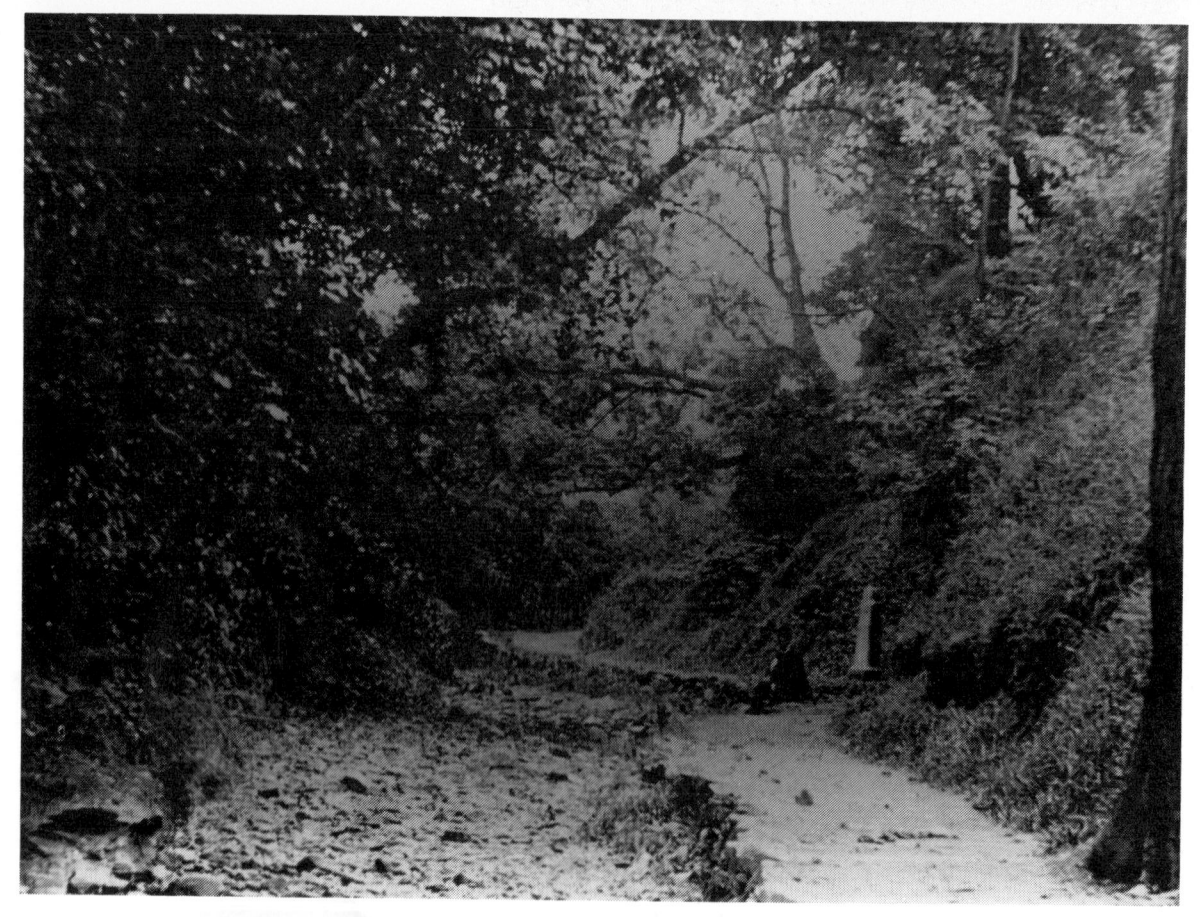

12. A quiet seat beside the Borgie Well memorial stone, dated 1879.

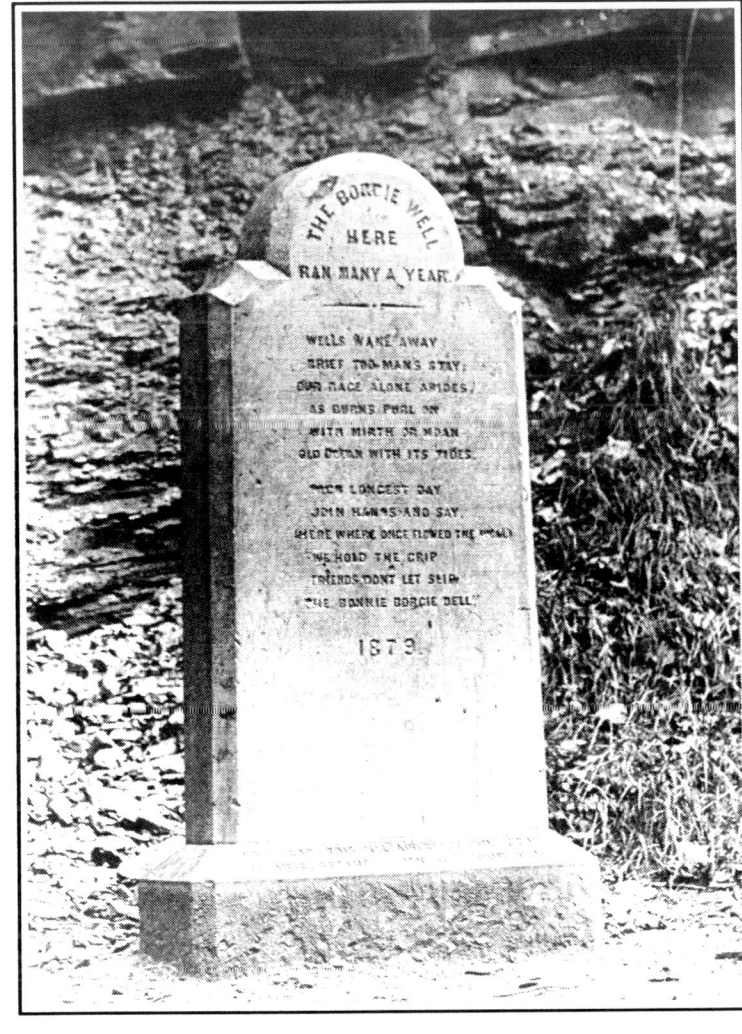

13. The inscription on the Borgie Well stone reads:

*The Borgie Well here,
Ran many a year.*

*Wells wane away
Brief too - man's stay;
Our race alone abides.
As burns purl on
With mirth or moan
Old ocean with its tides.*

*Pace longest day
Join hands and say,
(Here where once flowed the well)
"We hold the grip
Friends don't let slip
The Bonnie Borgie Dell".*

1879

*Come guard this dell and guard this stone
Because, because, both are your own.*

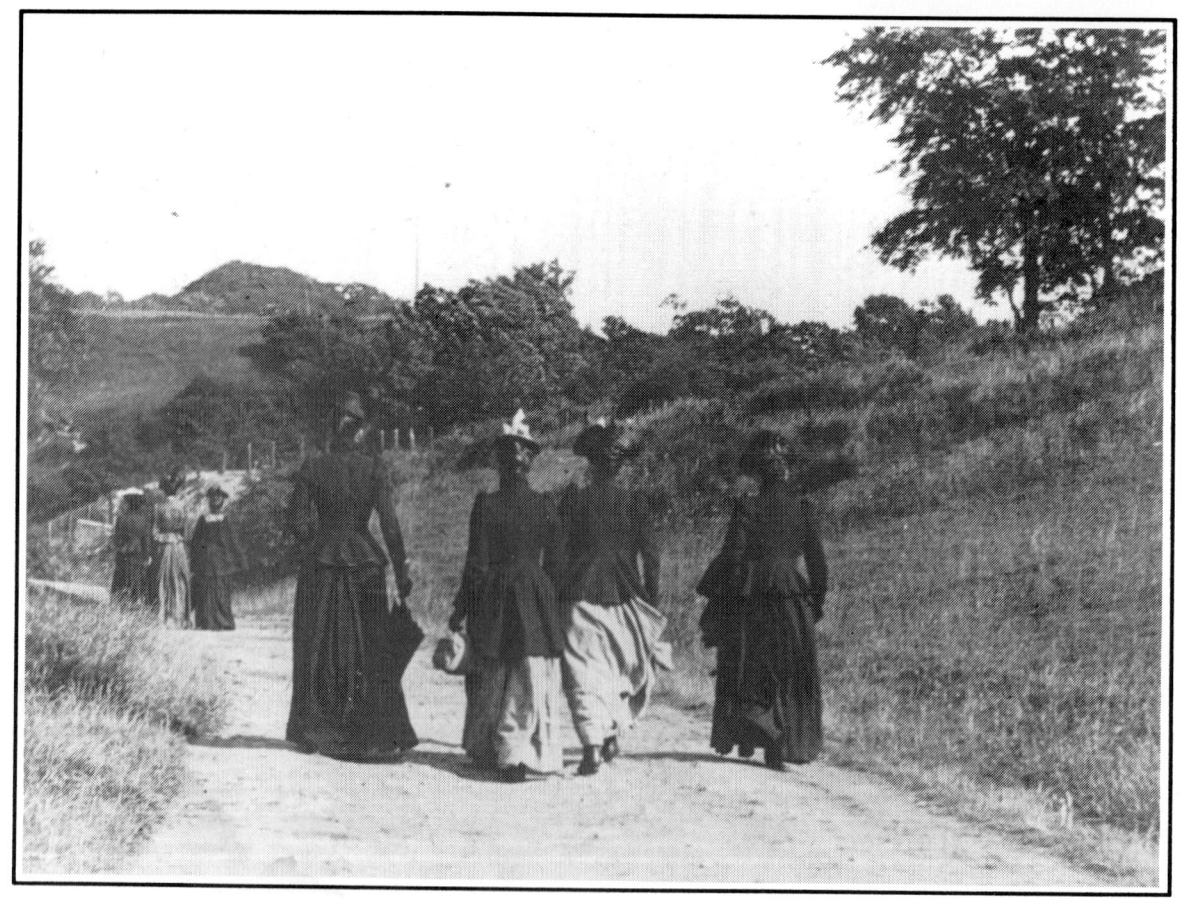

14. These elegant ladies are seen in 1892 going to the concert in the Borgie Glen, Cambuslang. The Borgie Glen was 13 acres in extent and embraced the historic Preaching Braes.

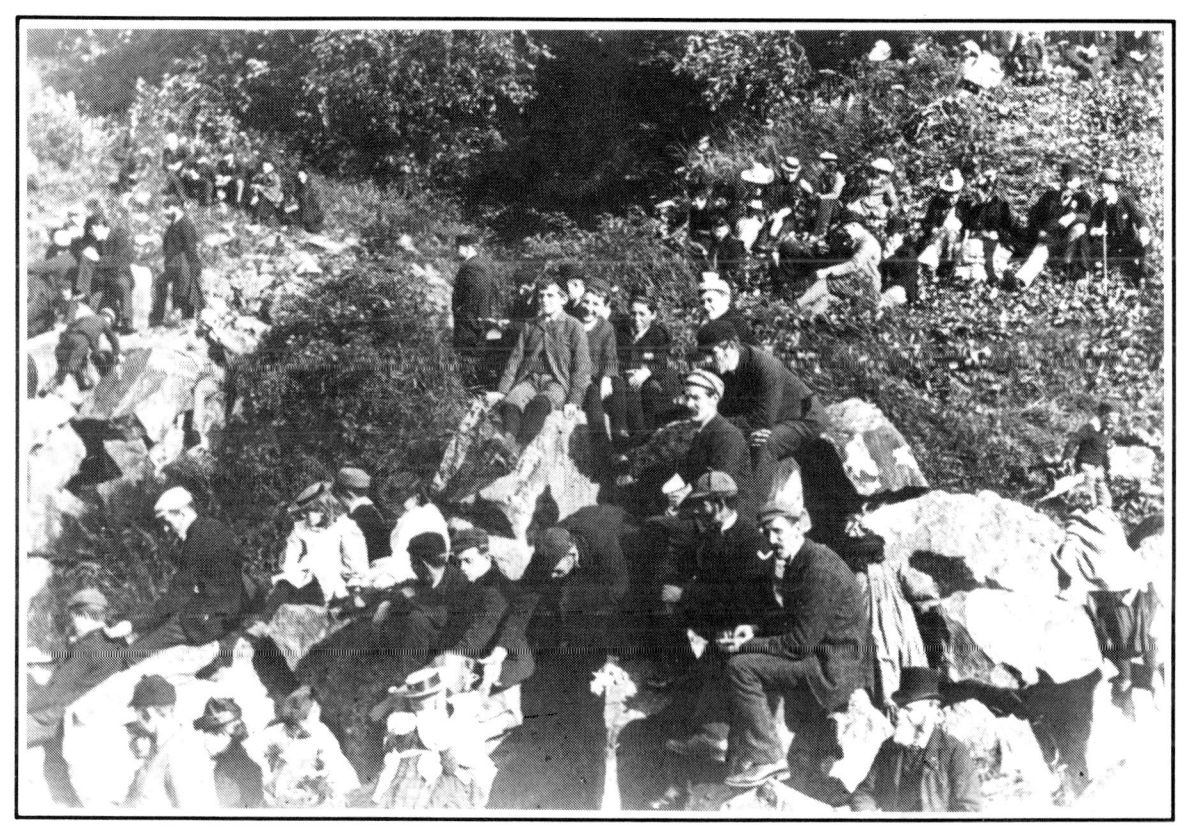

15. Musical enthusiasts in the audience at the concert in the Borgie Glen, 1892. The slope of the ground formed a natural amphitheatre.

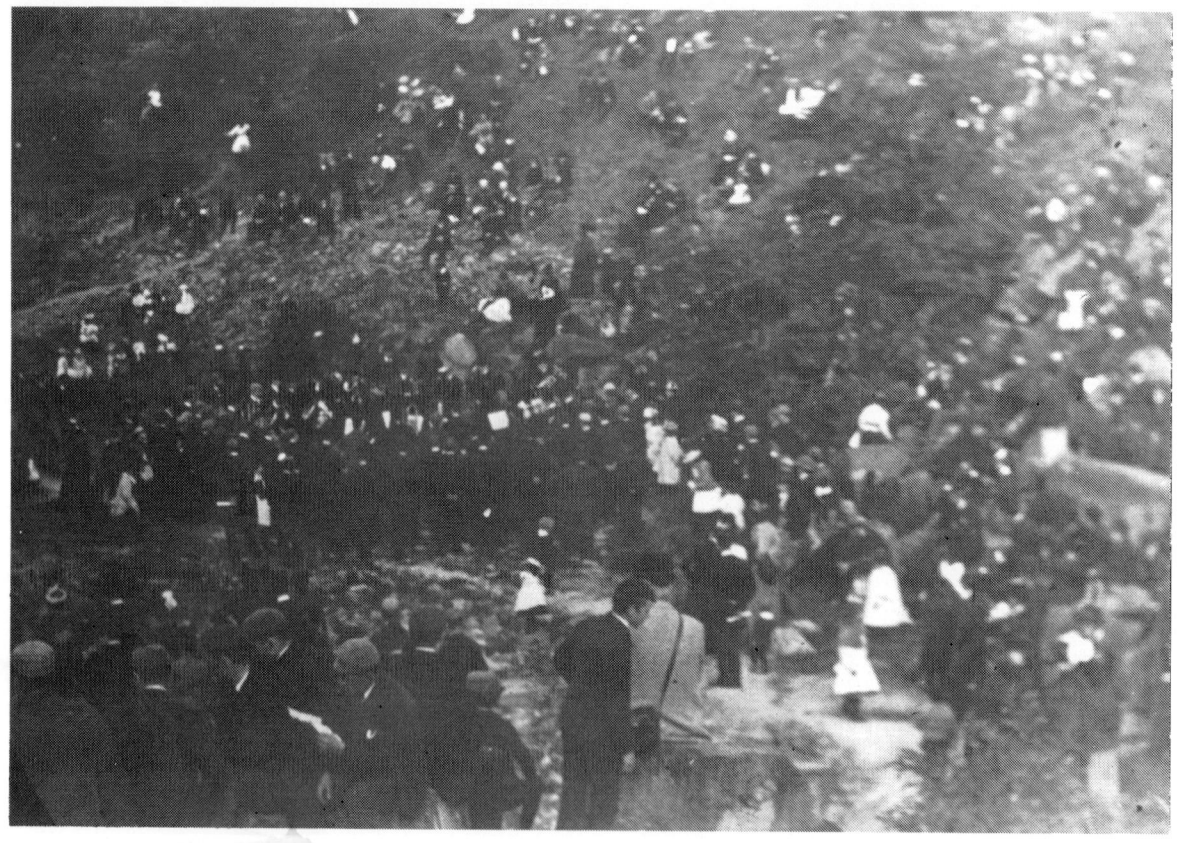

16. This scene in the 1890's depicts the Preaching Braes, with the masses gathered for an open-air assembly. The original area of the Preaching Braes covered thirteen acres. The Cambuslang "Wark" in 1742 went on for seven months and the preacher Mr Whitefield estimated that on 15 August the multitude reached upwards of 30,000.

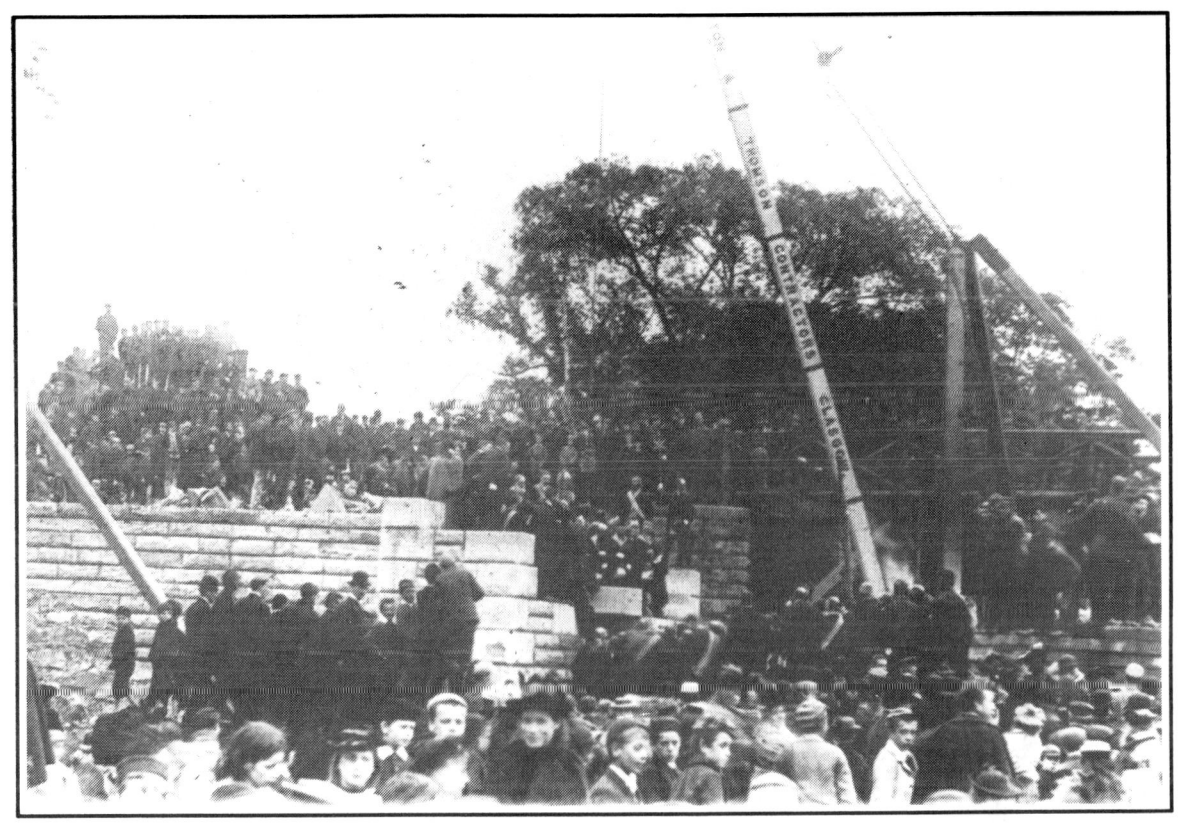

17. Crowds gathered at the Clyde Bridge under construction to witness the laying of the foundation stone (1892) with full Masonic honours by Mr R King Stewart of Murdostoun. The Cambuslang Trades Band headed the procession. The site was a little to the west of the Clyde Iron Company's railway bridge near the west end of Cambuslang.

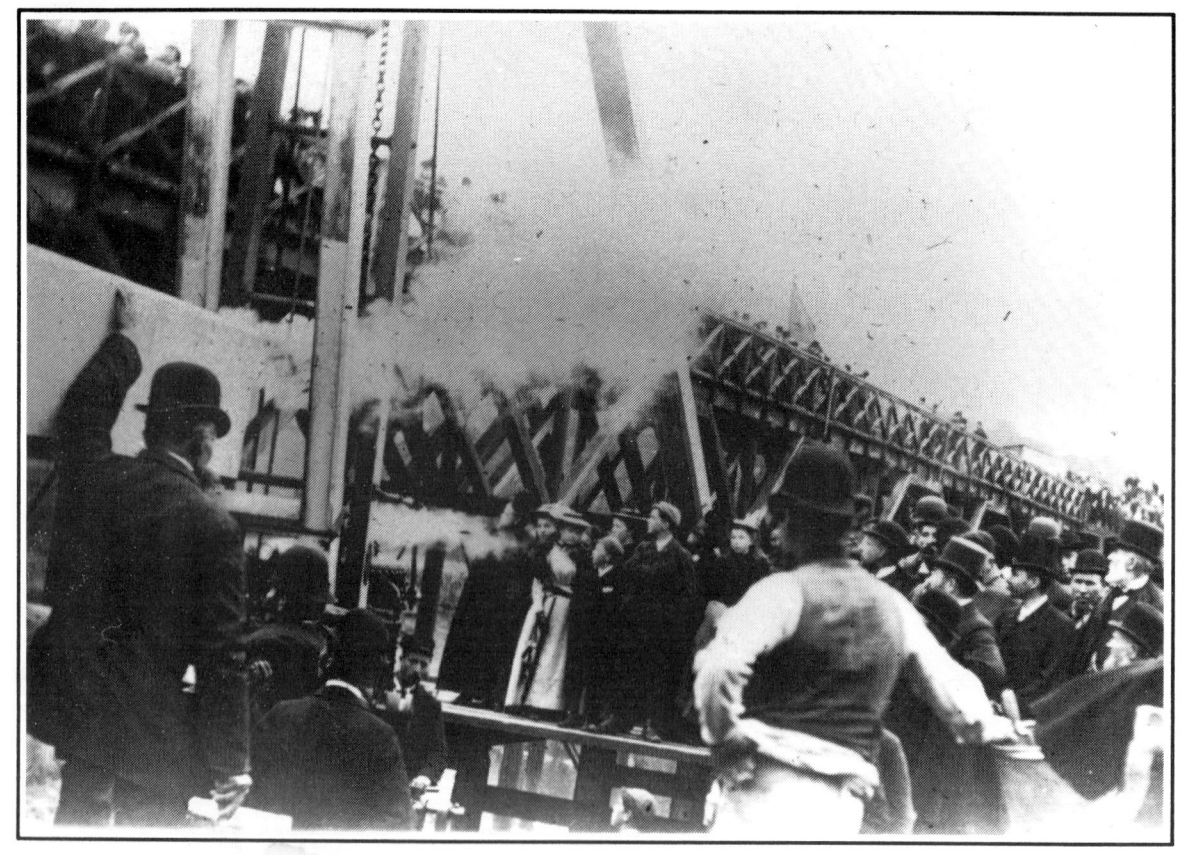

18. The scene at the Clyde Bridge in 1892 shows a large company assembled to sing and celebrate the building of the first bridge for vehicular traffic connecting Cambuslang with the north side of the river for speedy communications.

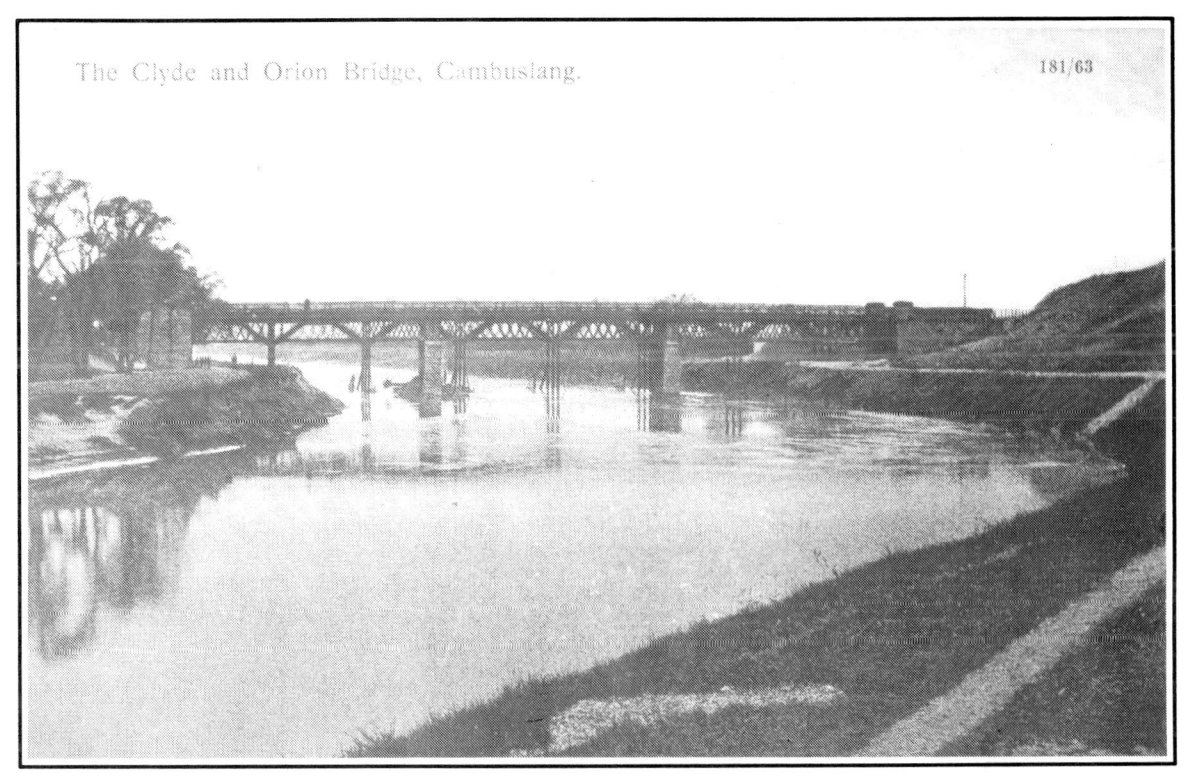

19. Side by side with the new Clyde Bridge constructed 1892, was the old Orion Bridge opened 1850, which was used for railway traffic in connection with the Clyde Ironworks. The Orion Bridge was burned down in 1919. The Clyde Bridge was the only vehicular bridge between Bothwell and Dalmarnock.

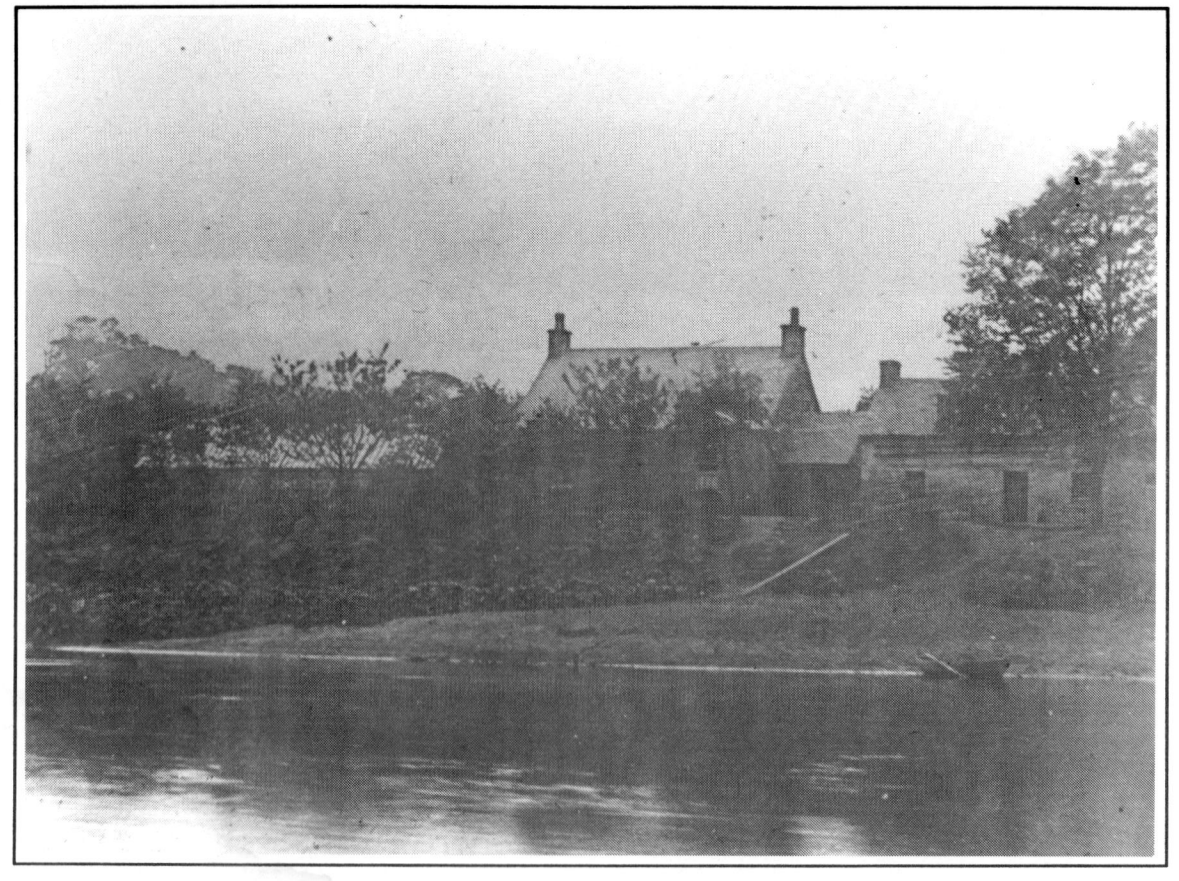

20. Prior to the erection of the new Clyde Bridge opened in 1892, fords were in daily use at Cambuslang but this mode of crossing was impracticable and necessitated traffic to Tollcross and Shettleston following a circuitous route. Trade and population had increased and it was a great inconvenience. The rowing boat from the Morriston Boat-house as seen in the 1890's might have given a lift across the river.

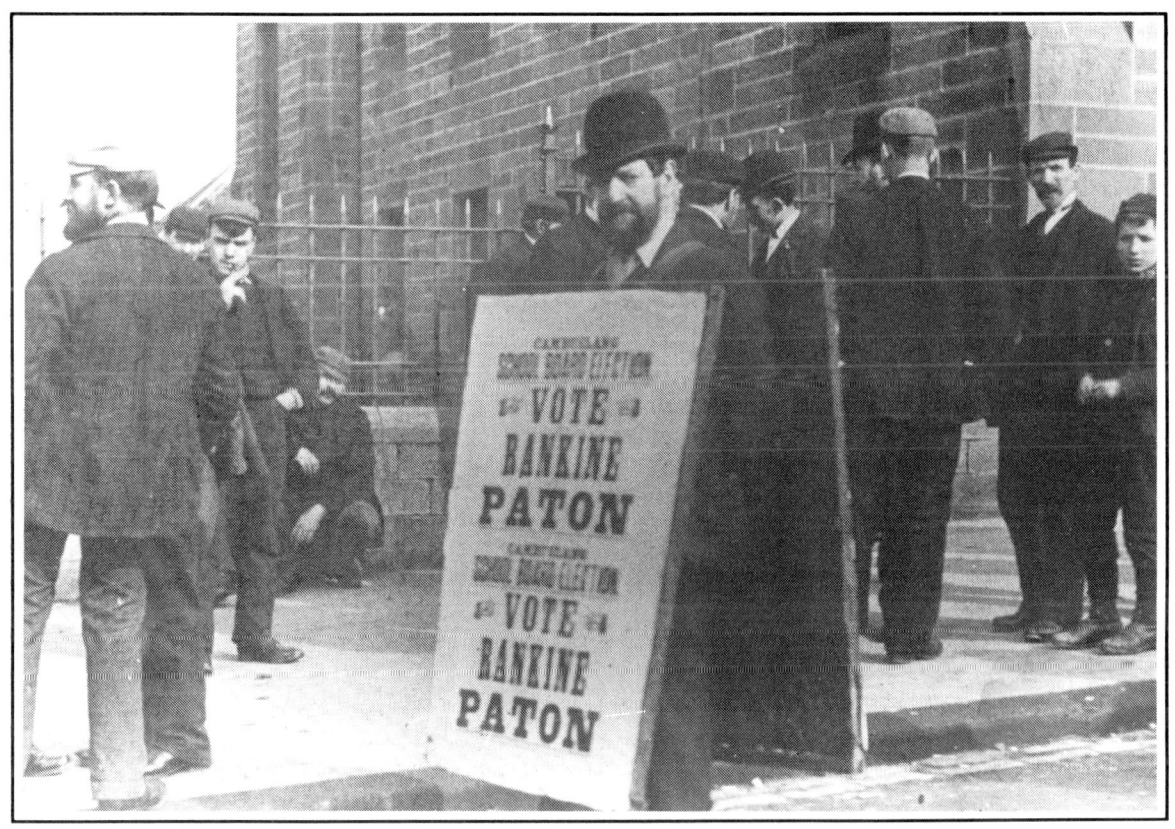

21. Crowds seen gathering in the 1890's outside Cambuslang Public School for the Triennial School Board Election. There was plenty to shout about as, although elementary school fees had been abolished in 1892, there were still the vexed questions of paying for books and the paying of fees in Higher Grade Schools.

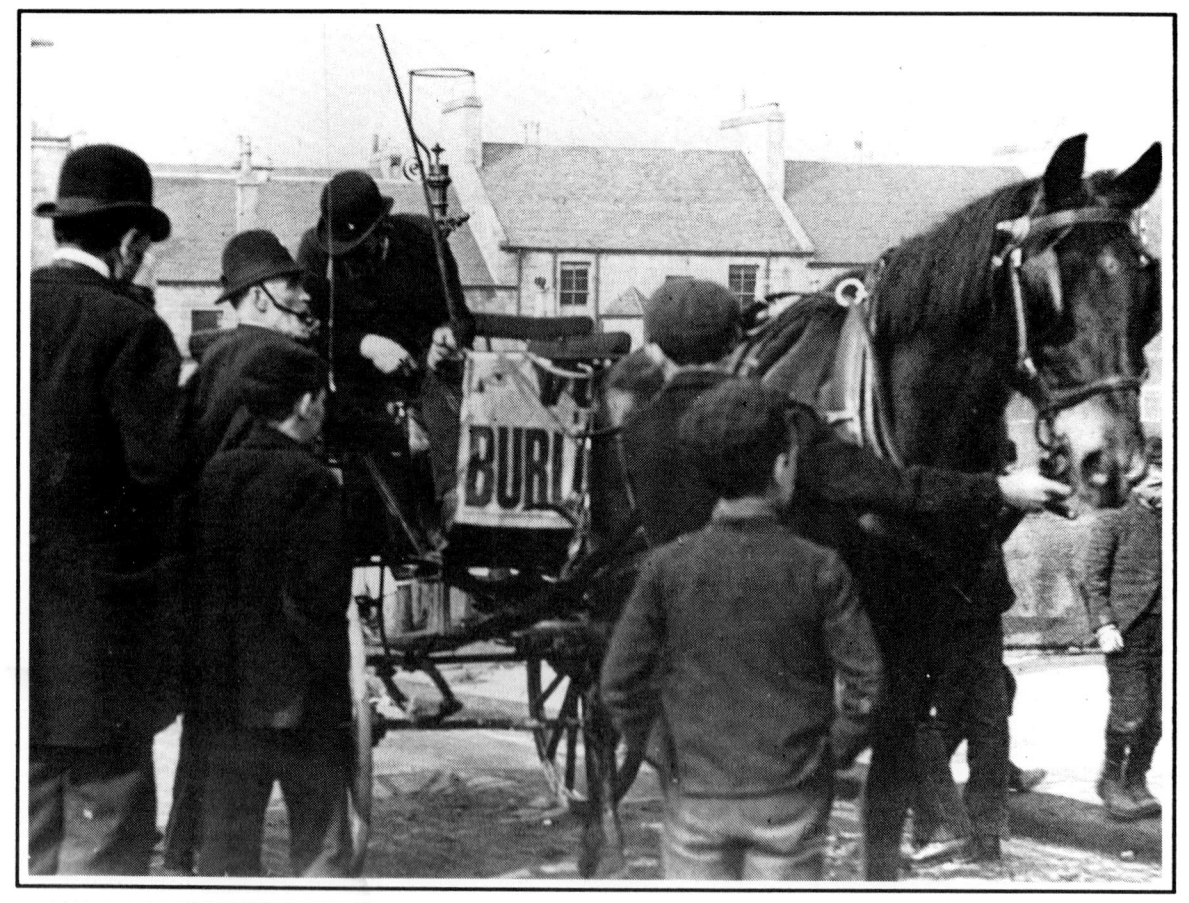

22. A horse and carriage in the 1890's seen engaged in electioneering. The committee men were ferreting out supporters and conveying auld wifies to the polling station. The children were given a holiday from school and were looking for the job of holding the horse's reins.

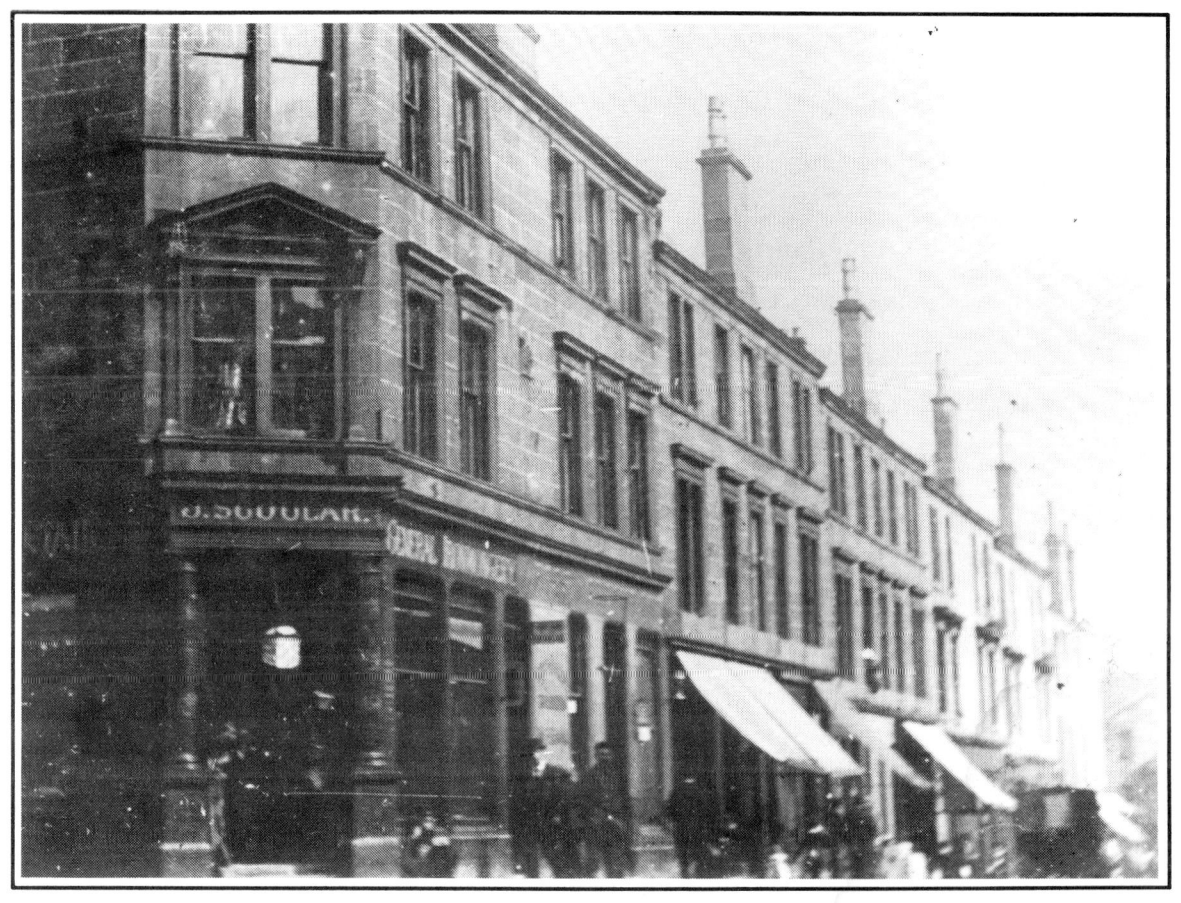

23. Scoular's Corner seen in the 1890's - Scoular's Ironmongery had a large key hanging in the doorway. Scoular's Smithy was in Hamilton Road.

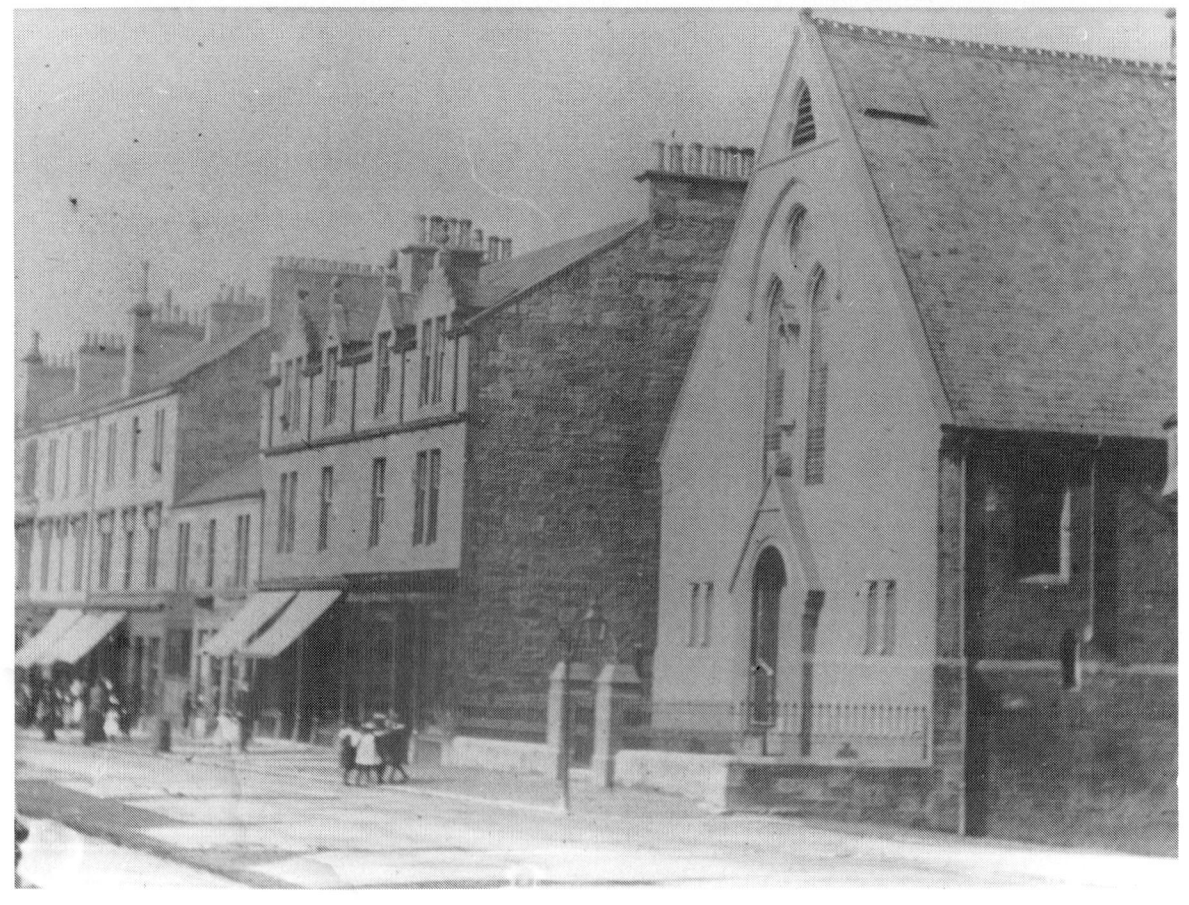

24. The Congregational Church was opened in 1875 in Main Street/Bank Street. The minister until 1895 was Reverend Thomas Brisbane. It was the oldest Congregational Church in Lanarkshire, originating in a rented house in 1799 and then a chapel at the east end of Tabernacle Street.

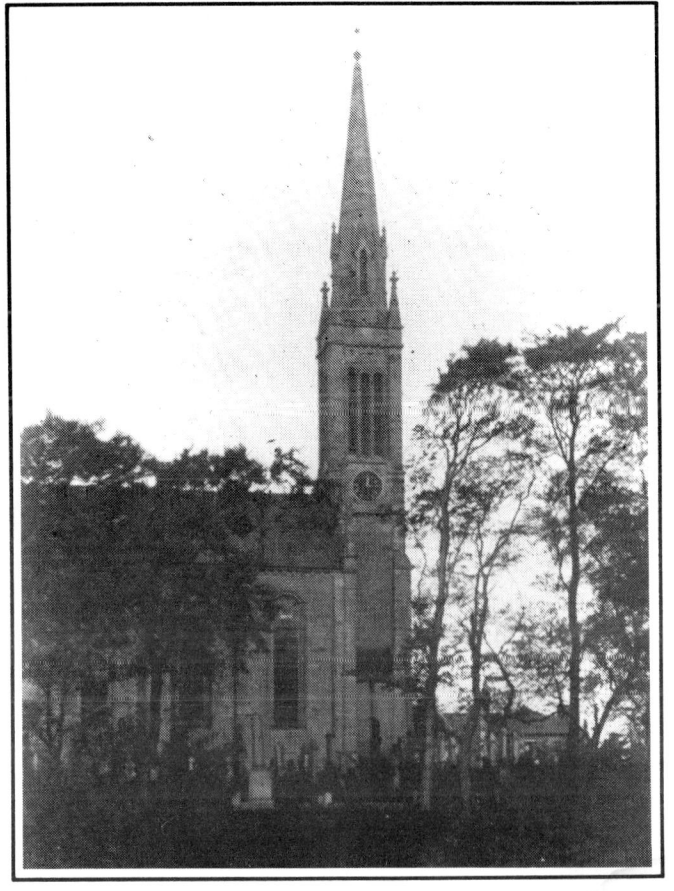

25. Cambuslang Old Parish Church was built in 1743 and was replaced by this fine building in 1841. The Reverend James S Johnson DD, performed the duties of parish minister for 38 years and was also chairman of the Cambuslang School Board from 1873 until his death in 1881.

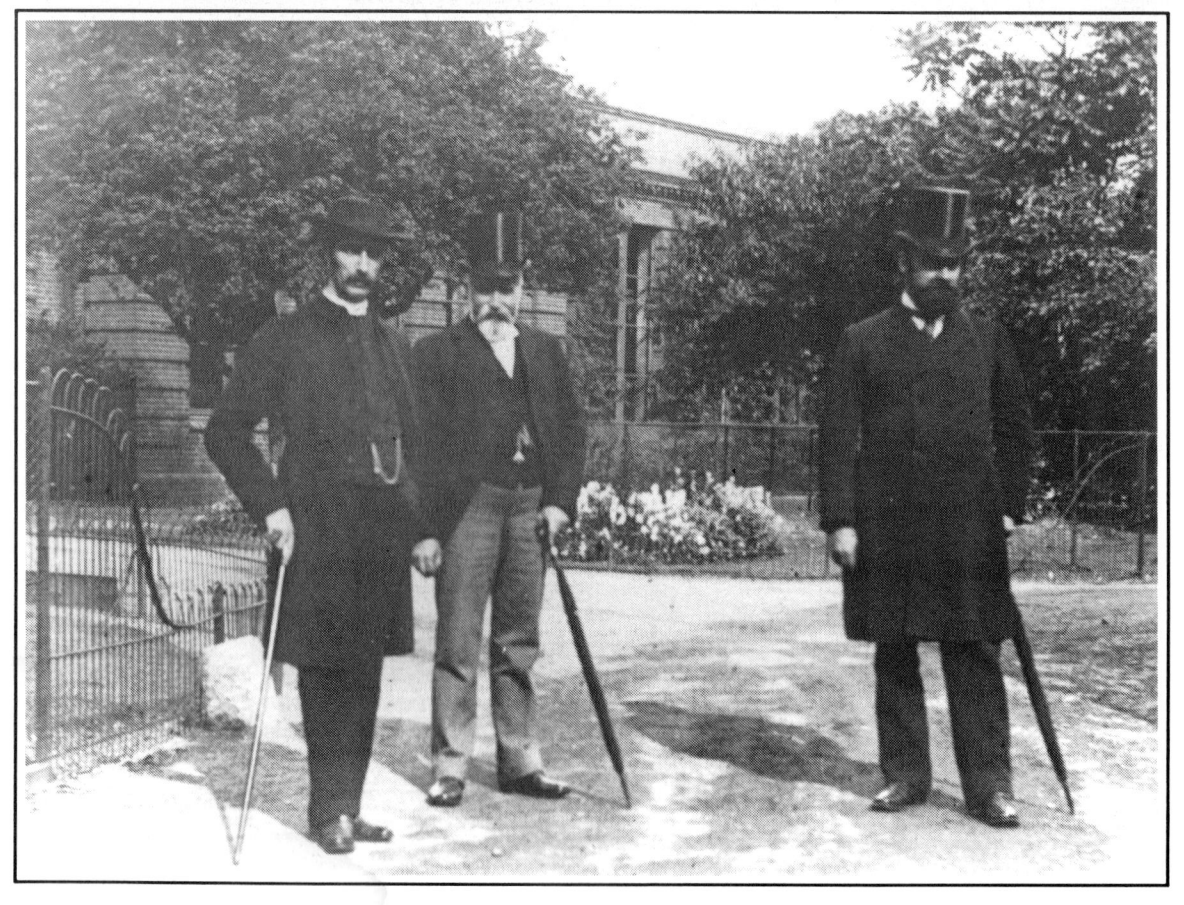

26. Purported to be Reverend Dr Johnston, Reverend Dr Robertson and Dr Meek in the 1890's.

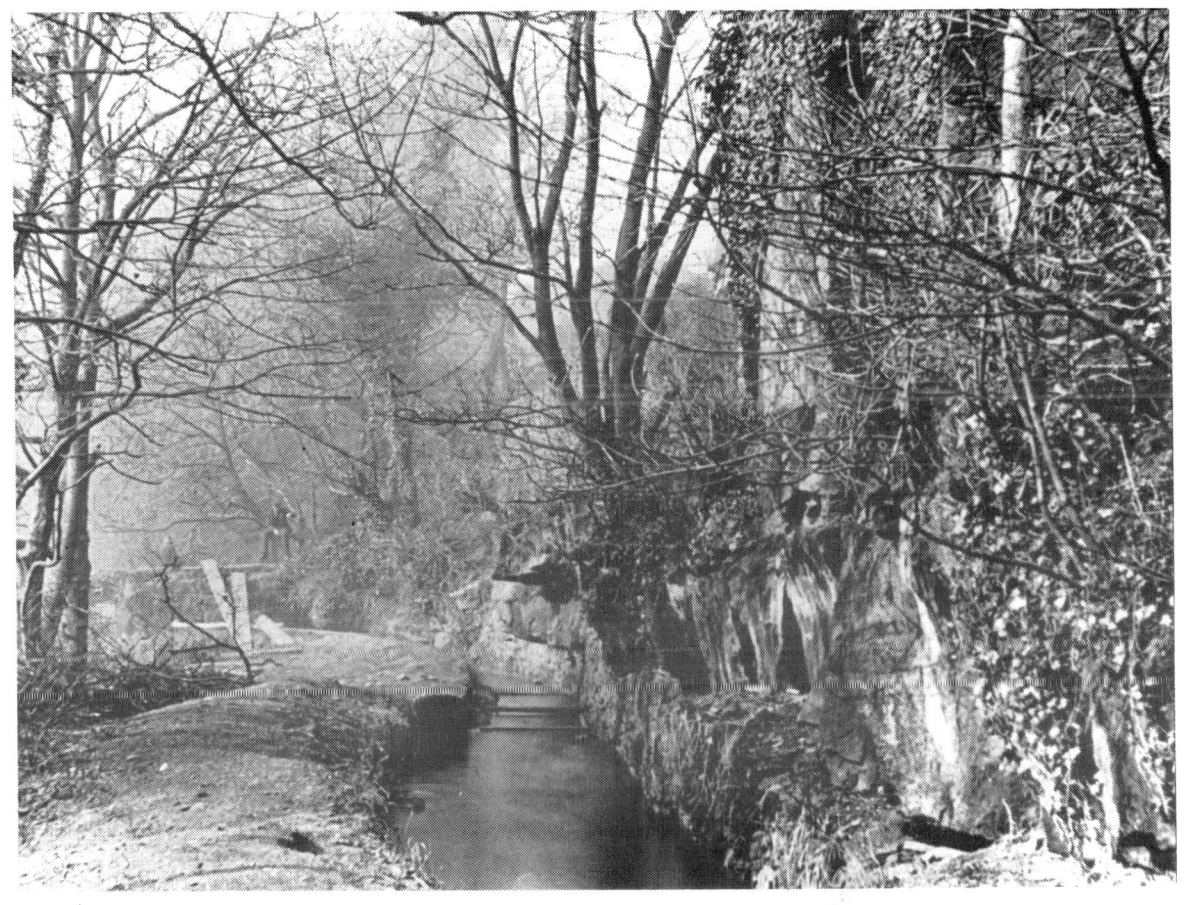

27. A man and child in the 1890's enjoy a quiet rest in the sylvan setting of Cambuslang Park, which was 14 acres in extent.

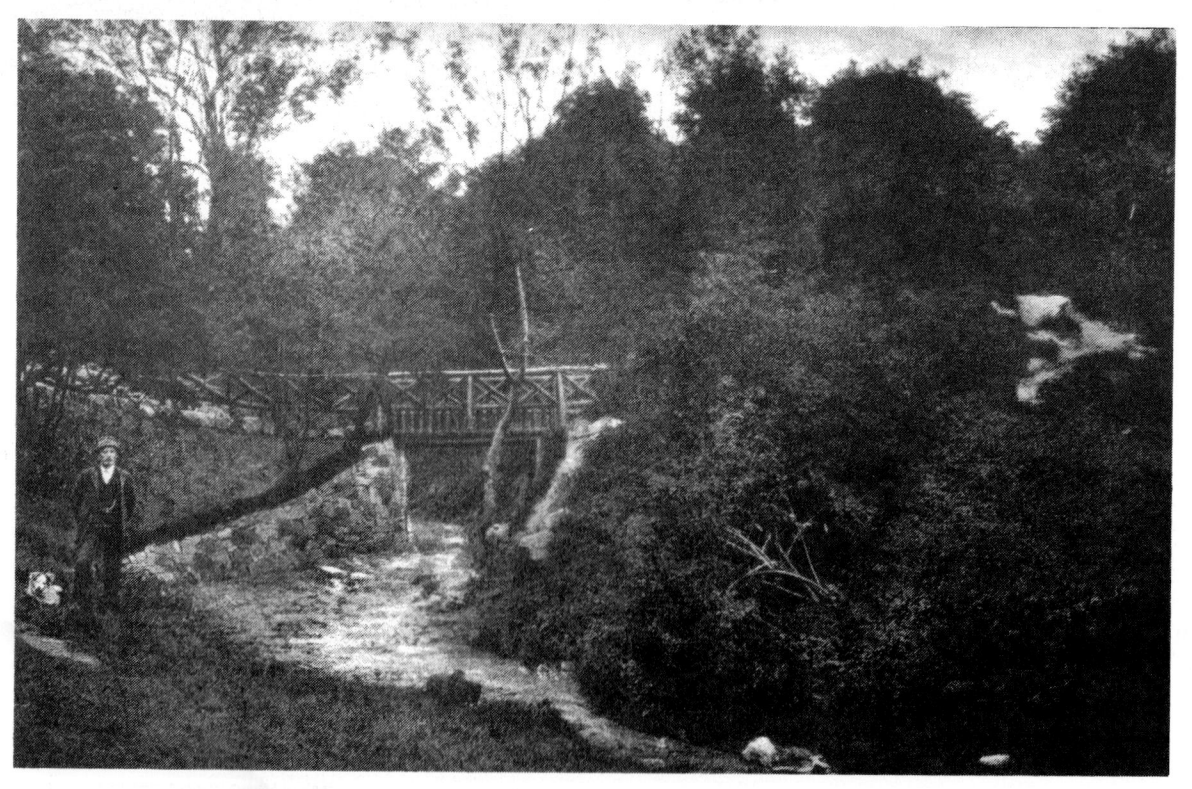

28. A view of the new Cambuslang Park which opened in 1913.

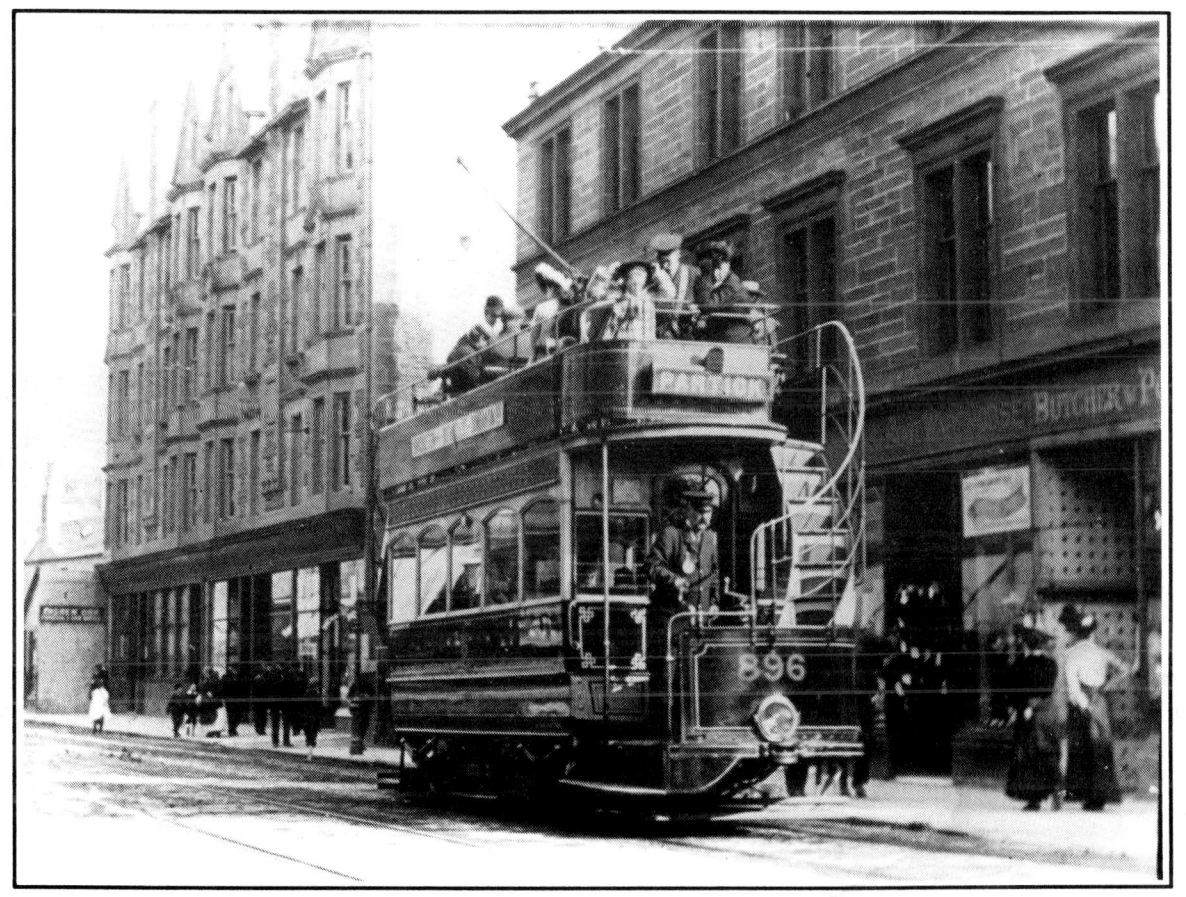

29. Tramcar No 896 of the Glasgow Tramways is making its way, c 1904, along Cambuslang Main Street, on its way to Bridgeton Cross and Partick. It was popular to 'get up them stairs and hold on to one's hat' to fully enjoy the open-air trip. Note the large Co-operative Building in the background.

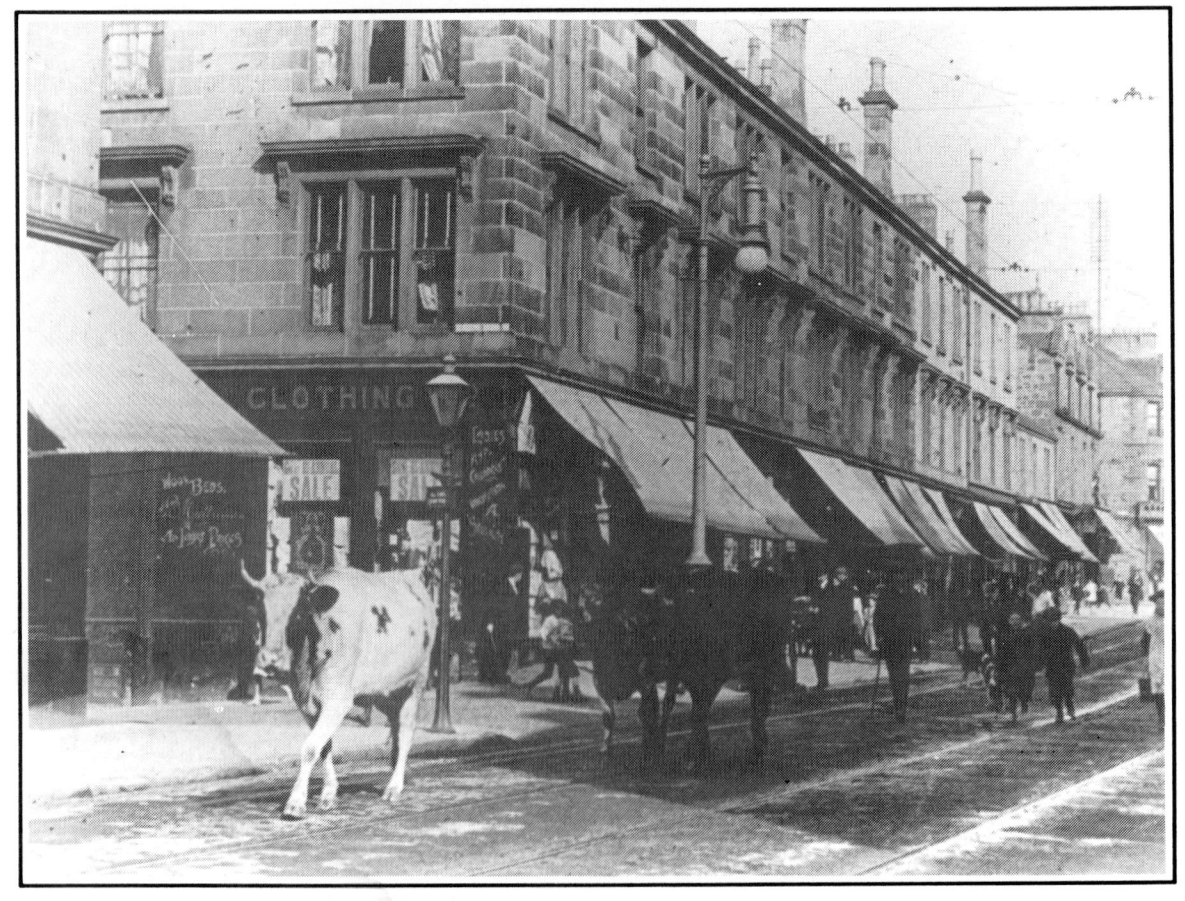

30. Cows walking leisurely along Main Street, Cambuslang at the turn of the century. The farms in the surrounding areas were mostly arable, but there was some grazing for sheep and cattle.

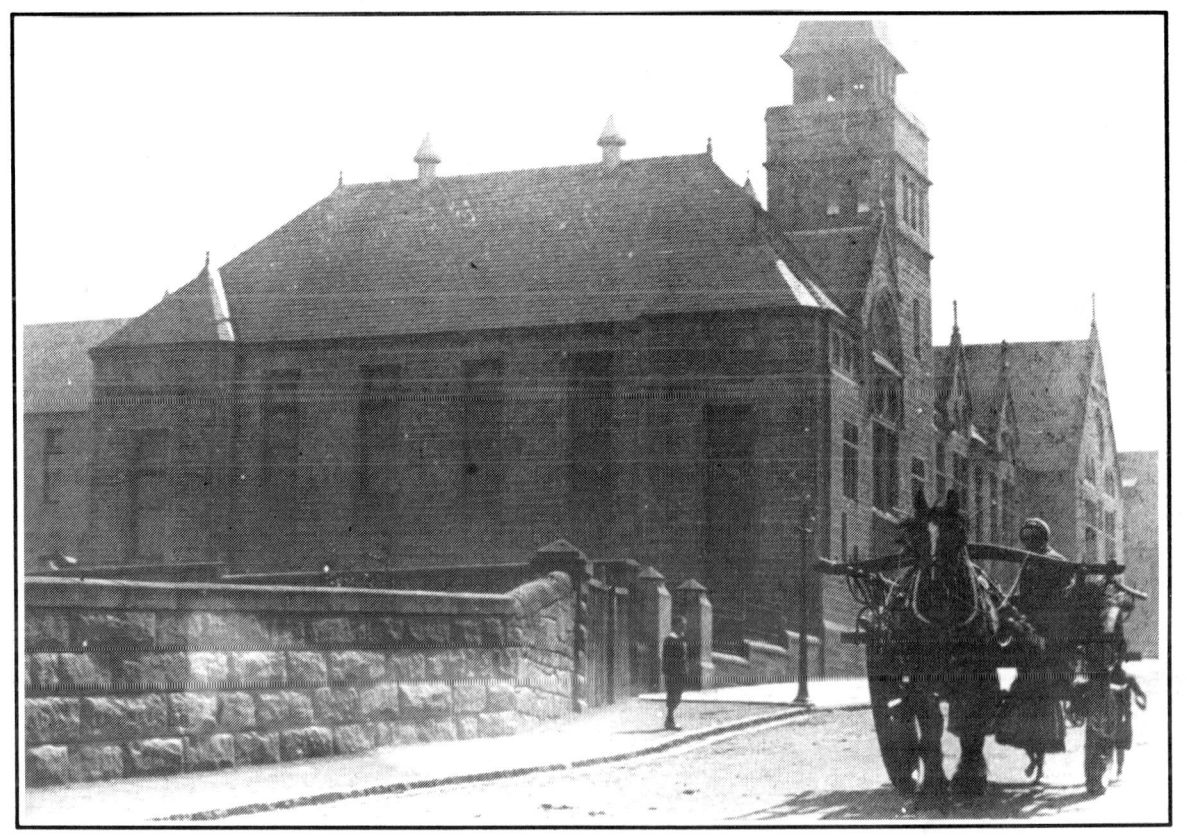

31. Cambuslang Public School at the corner of Greenlees Road/Tabernacle Street has the datestone 1882. It was styled by the School Board's architect, Mr A Lindsay Miller, with Gothic details, a square tower with spire within the parapet, and roundels. There were three extensions. The school closed in 1974 becoming an annexe to the School of Building. It is now a Nursing Home.

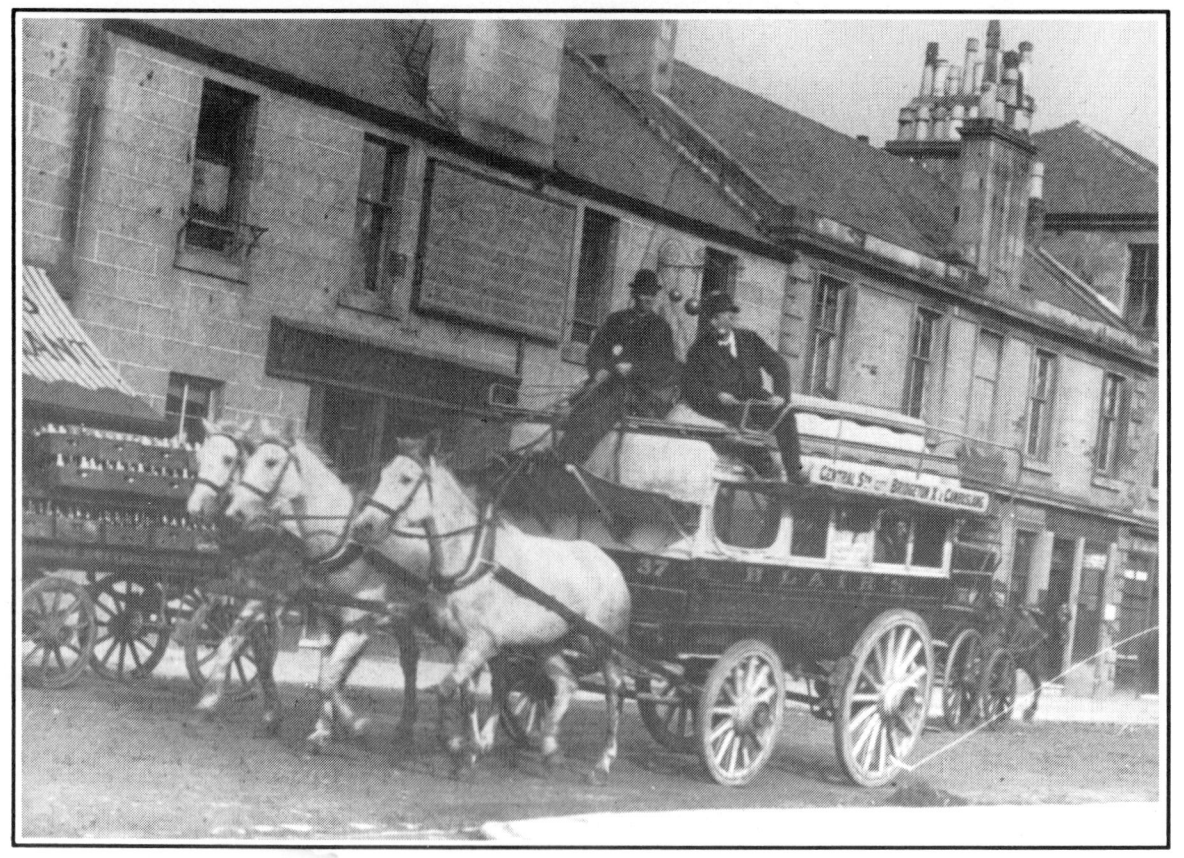

32. Blair's Bus proceeds along Main Street as seen in the 1890's. The service from Rutherglen to Bridgeton Cross was established in 1884 and was later extended. Service 37 was from Cambuslang to Central Station. The buses were withdrawn in 1896. Note Hastie's Restaurant, the Loan Office and the pawnshop with its sign of the three brass balls.

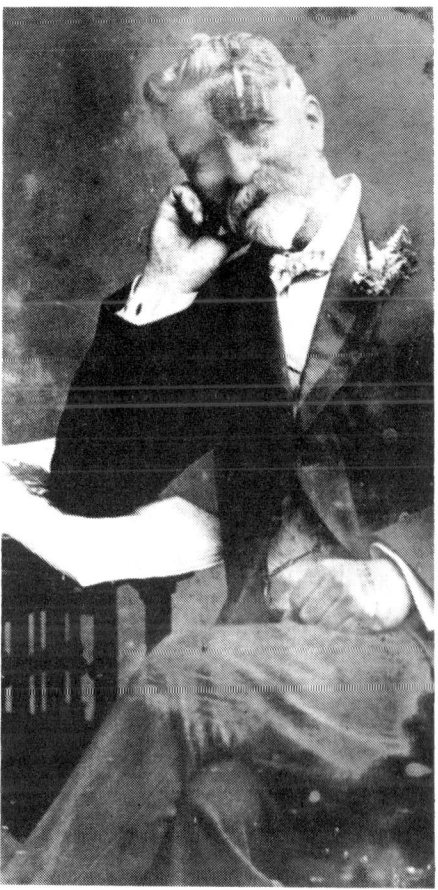

33. James Hastie, a remarkable man who set off on a bold venture, was born in 1843. After training as a baker, he borrowed five gold sovereigns from his father-in-law and started his own bakery delivering his goods in a hand-cart. Various premises were used including those in Main Street, Cambuslang near Church Street.

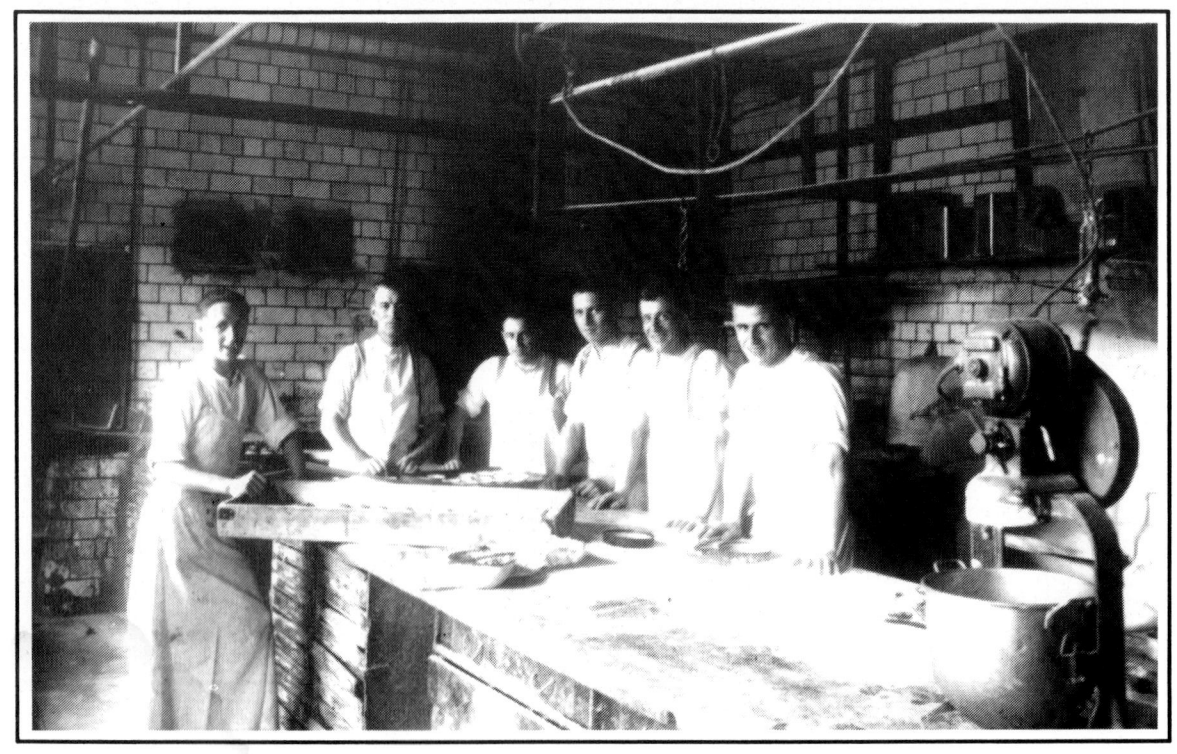

34. Bakery workers of James Hastie & Co pose on the premises of Morriston Street Bakery in the 1920's. Here the workers are seen in their protective clothing and using the 'hand-made' method. The bread was delivered by horse-drawn vehicles. The business is now managed by the fourth generation of the family.

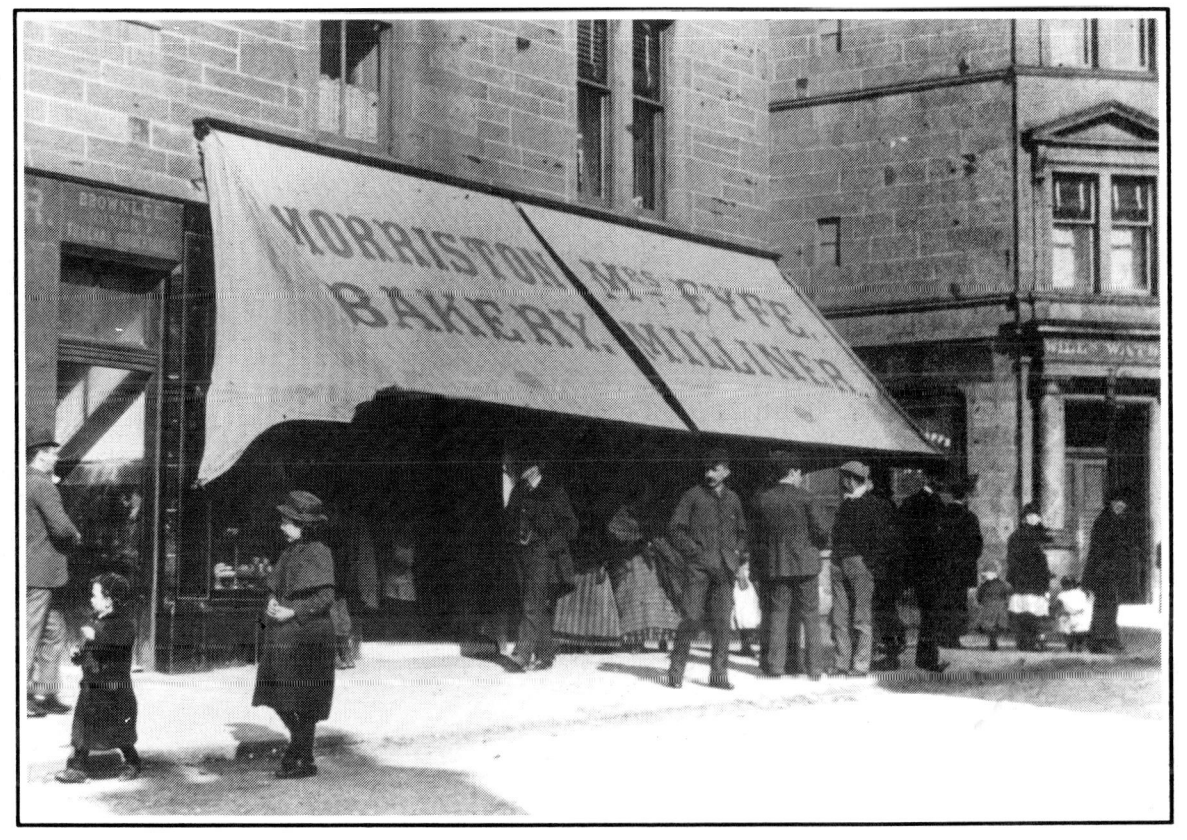

35. This scene depicts Main Street in the 1890's and shows Brownlee (Joiner and Funeral Undertaker), Hastie's bakery shop (Morriston Bakery) and Mrs Fyfe (Milliner).

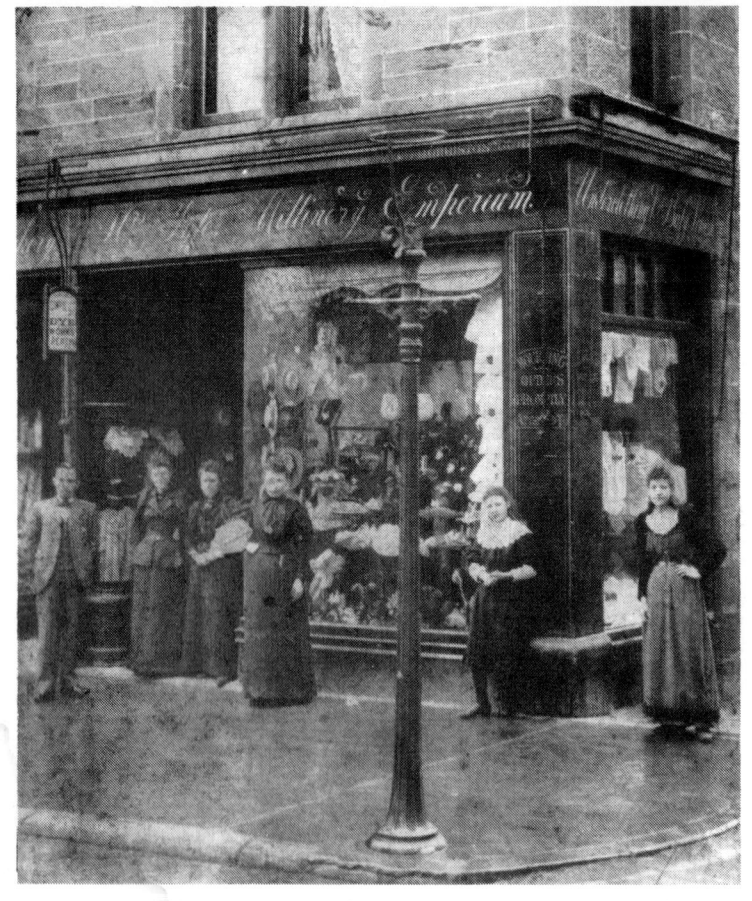

36. A closer view of Mrs Fyfe's Millinery Emporium which catered for a lifetime's clothing needs from baby linens to mourning orders. A fashionable staff would ensure you were being served. Note the sign for Campbells Dyeworks, Perth.

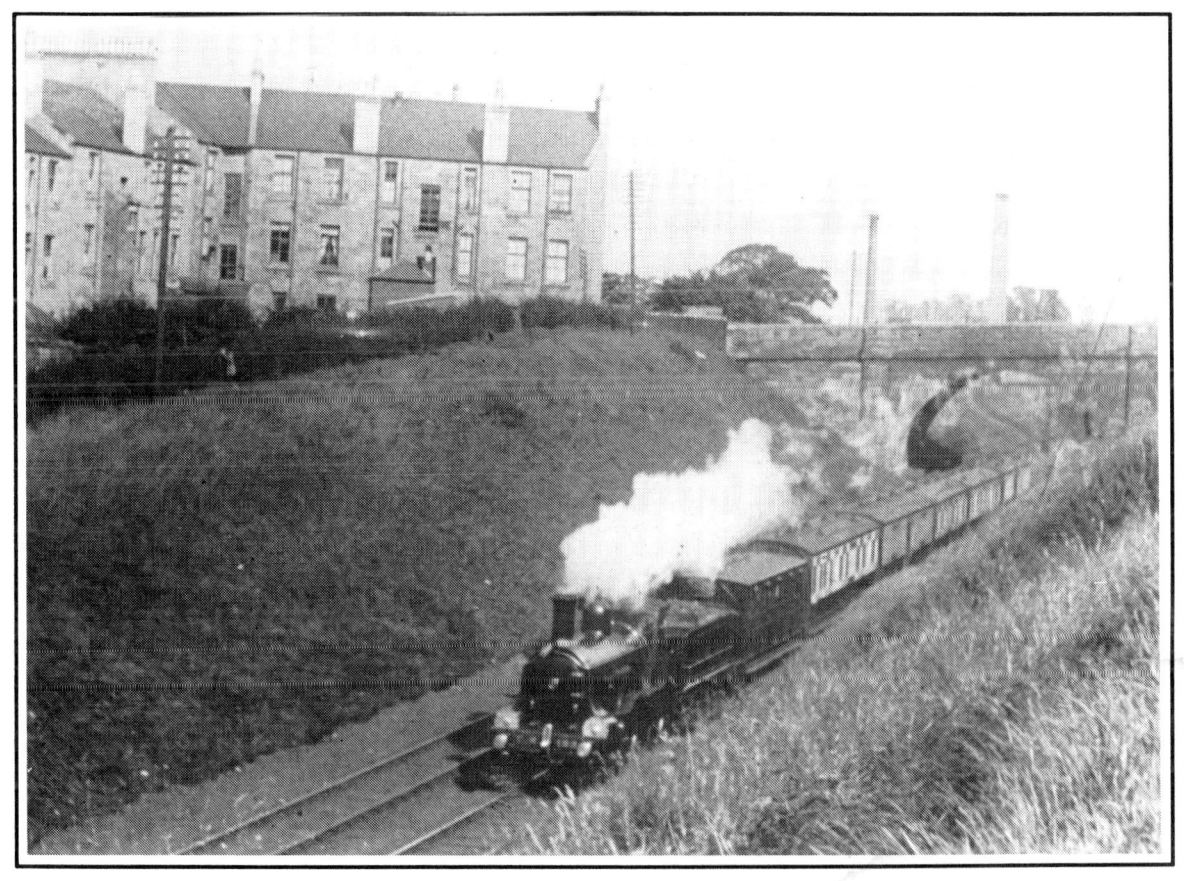

37. Clydesdale Junction Railway (Caledonian Railway) came with the construction of the railways in the area in 1845. Here seen in the 1890's is a train of the Caledonian Railway, steaming along behind Cambuslang Main Street and approaching Cambuslang Station.

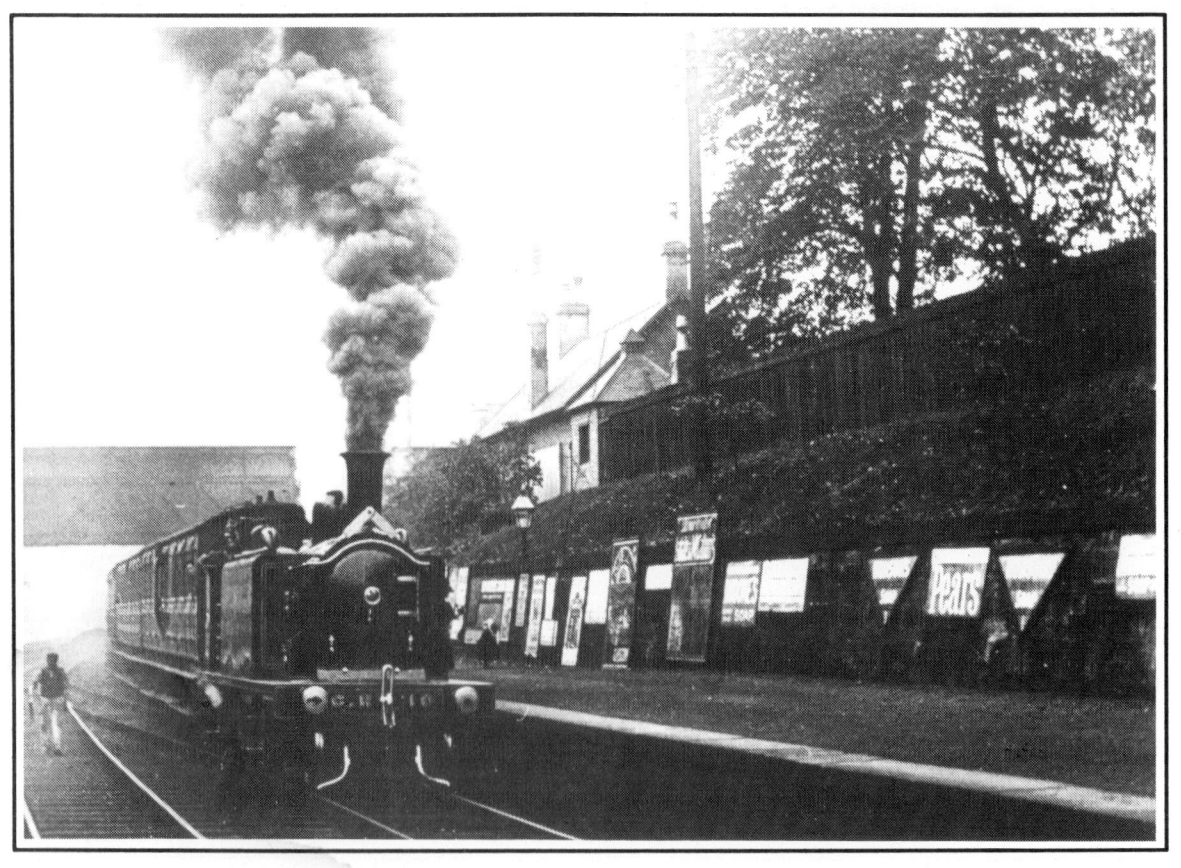

38. Caledonian Railway locomotive No 10 as seen at Cambuslang Station at the turn of the century. The station opened in 1881. Note the advertisements for Pears soap and Hudsons soap.

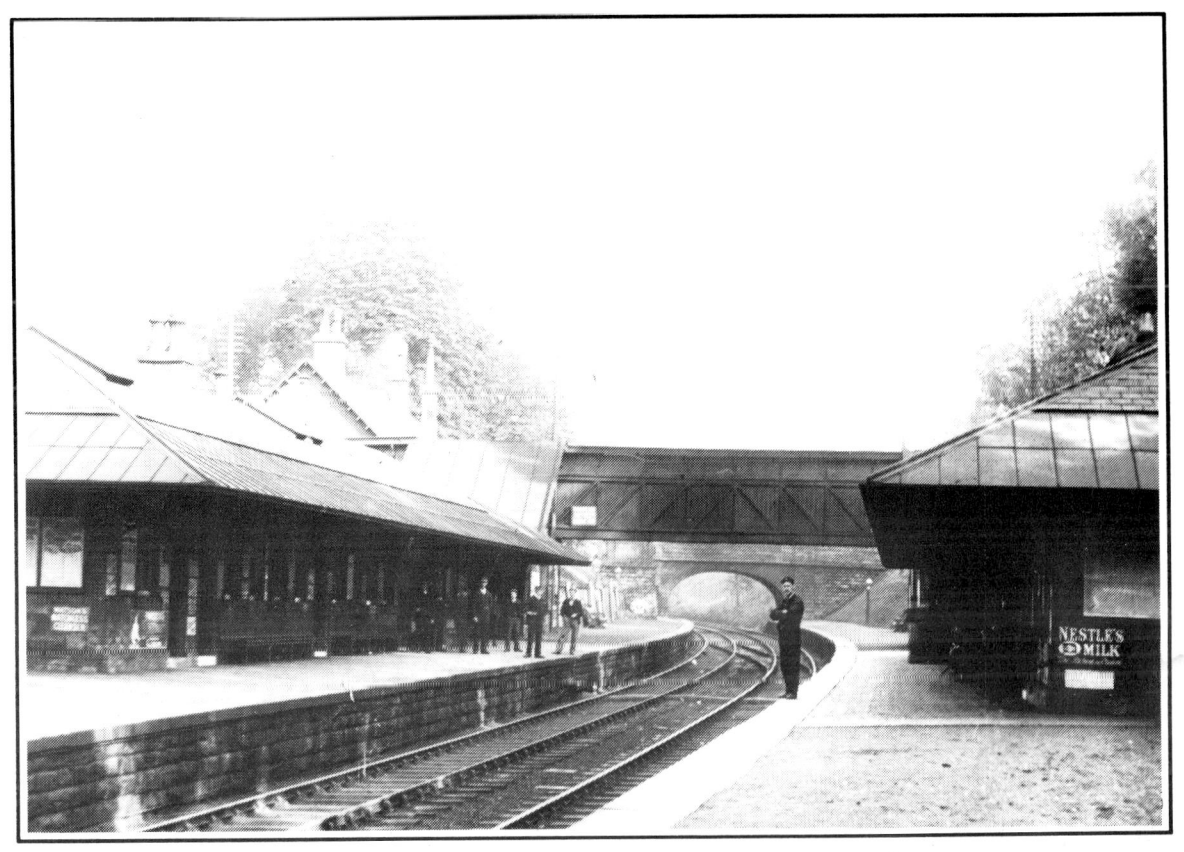

39. A large complement of Railway Staff at Cambuslang Station as seen in the 1890's. The station could be flooded out with excursions and 3,000 extra tickets were issued in one day.

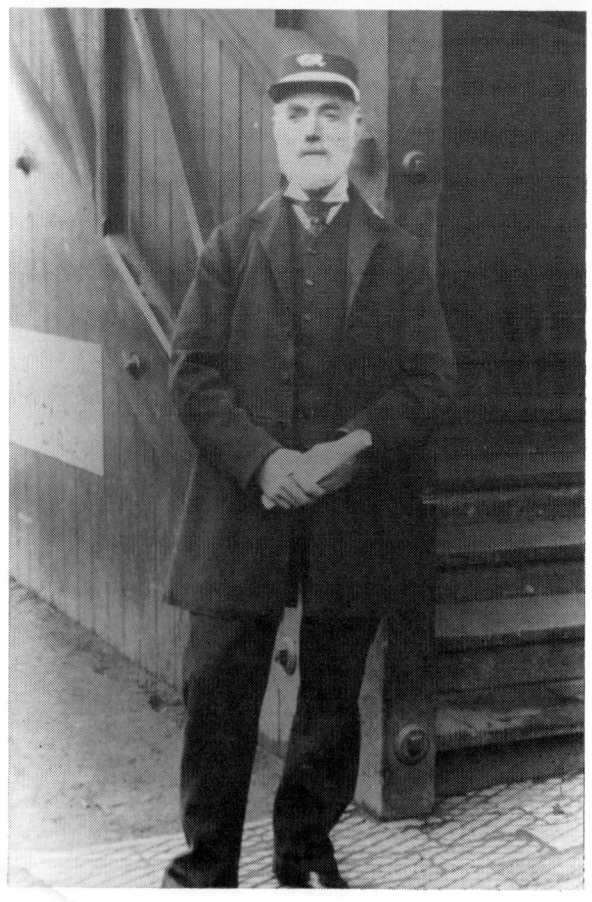

40. This is purported to be Andrew McLachlan, Railway Station Master, who lived at the Turnpike Road Railway Station House. The location is Cambuslang Station in the 1890's and he is wearing the uniform of the Caledonian Railway, rather drab and not a brass button to be seen.

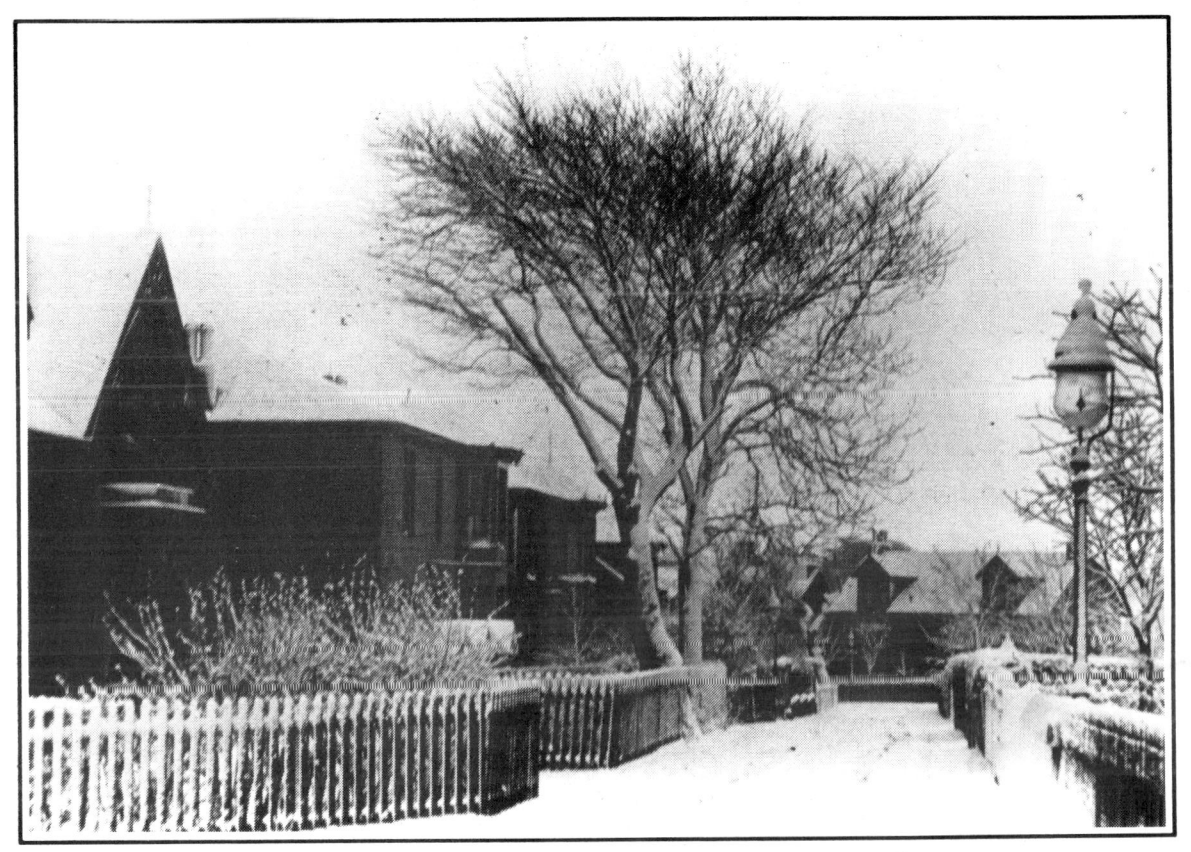

41. A pre 1900 Central Avenue winter scene.

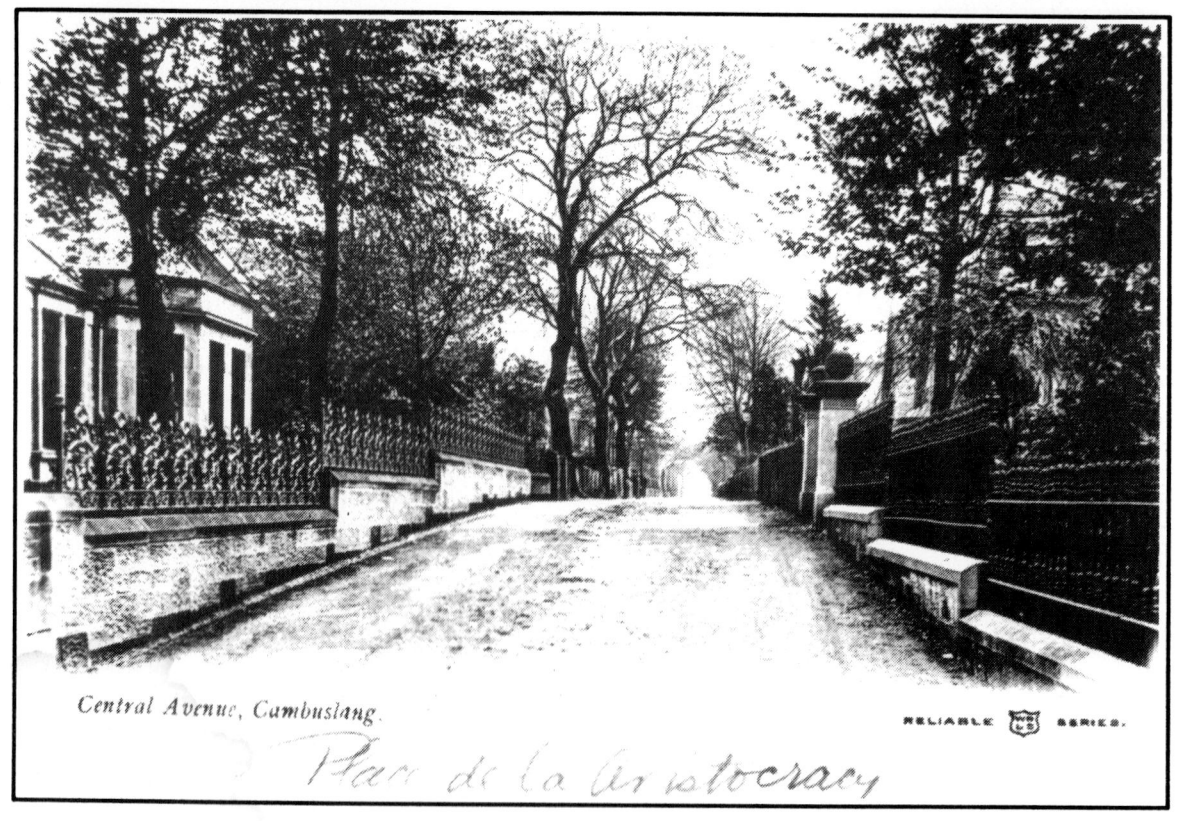

Central Avenue, Cambuslang.

Place de la Aristocracy

42. Central Avenue after the turn of the century. It is interesting that the sender of the postcard wrote "Place de l'aristocracy". The west end of Central Avenue was at Wellshot (mid) lodge guarding Wellshot House owned by the Buchanans, feudal superiors of the nearby lands.

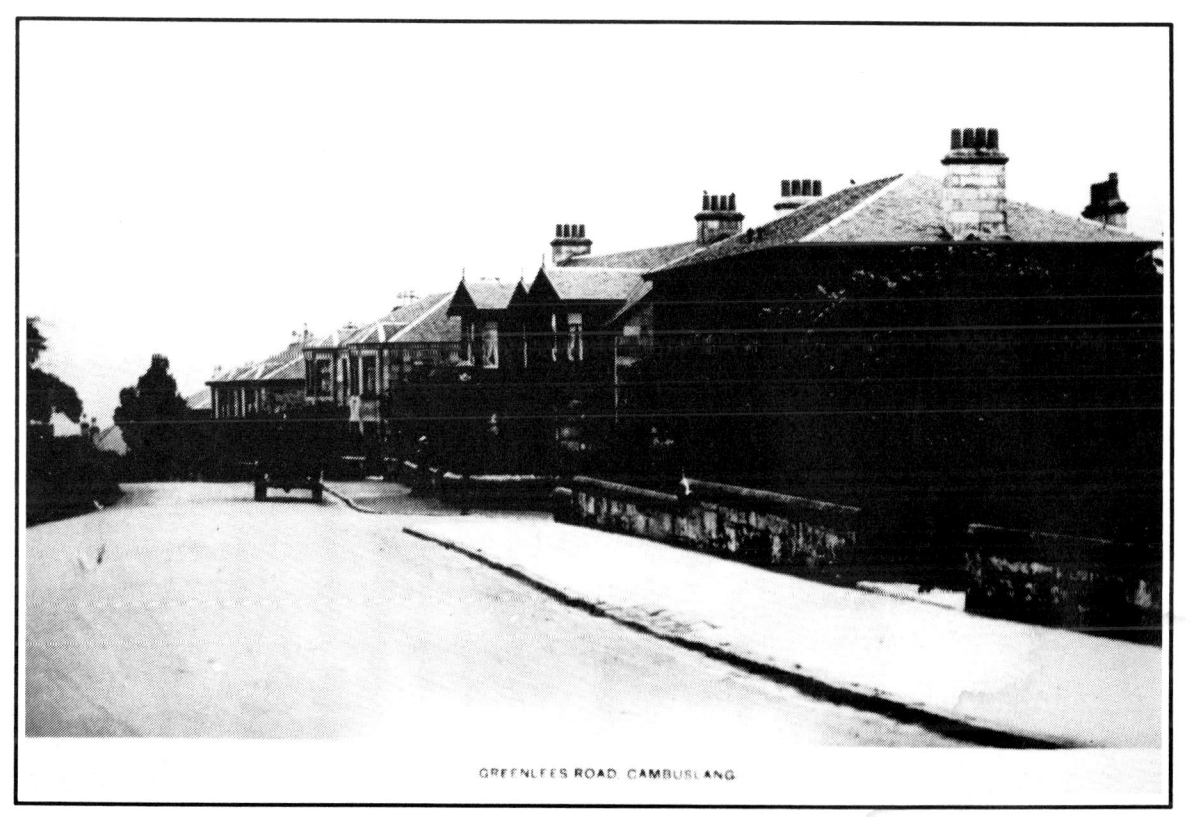

43. A peaceful Greenlees Road pictured c 1910.

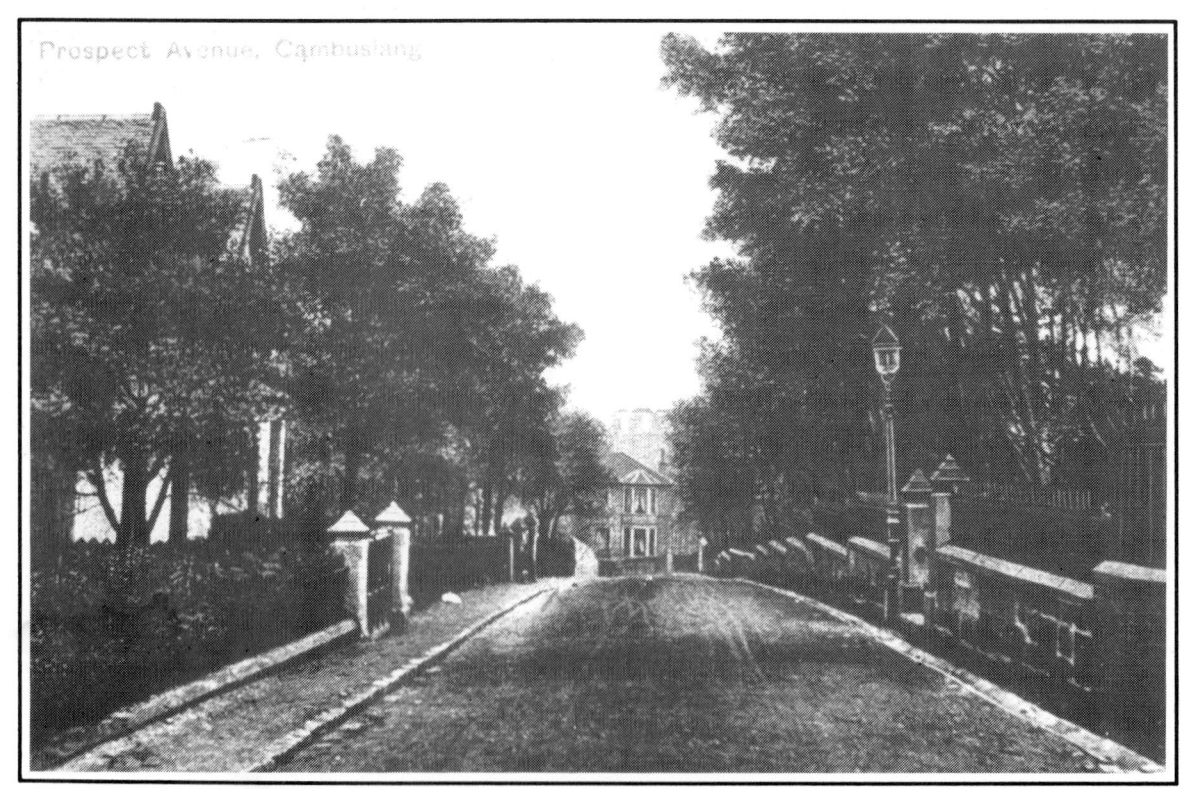

44. Prospect Avenue c 1905.

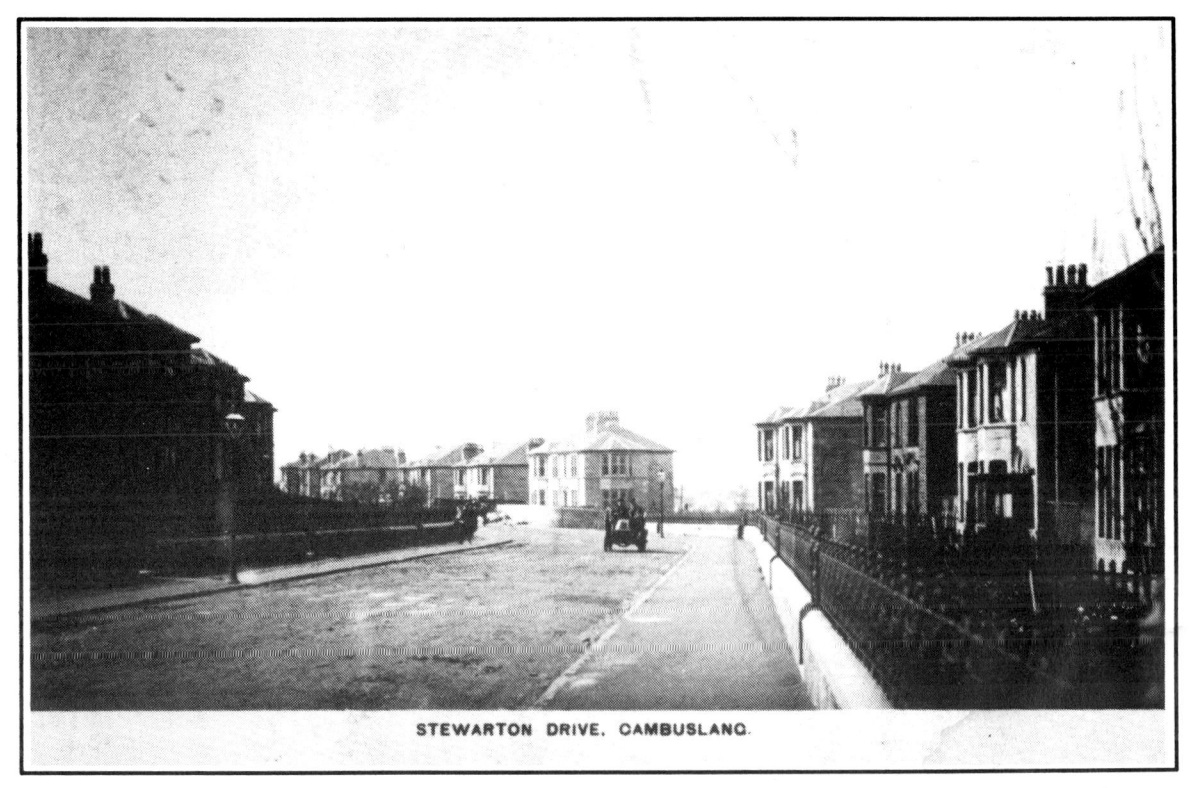

STEWARTON DRIVE, CAMBUSLANG.

45. Stewarton Drive is seen c 1910 with a motor-driven vehicle making good progress.

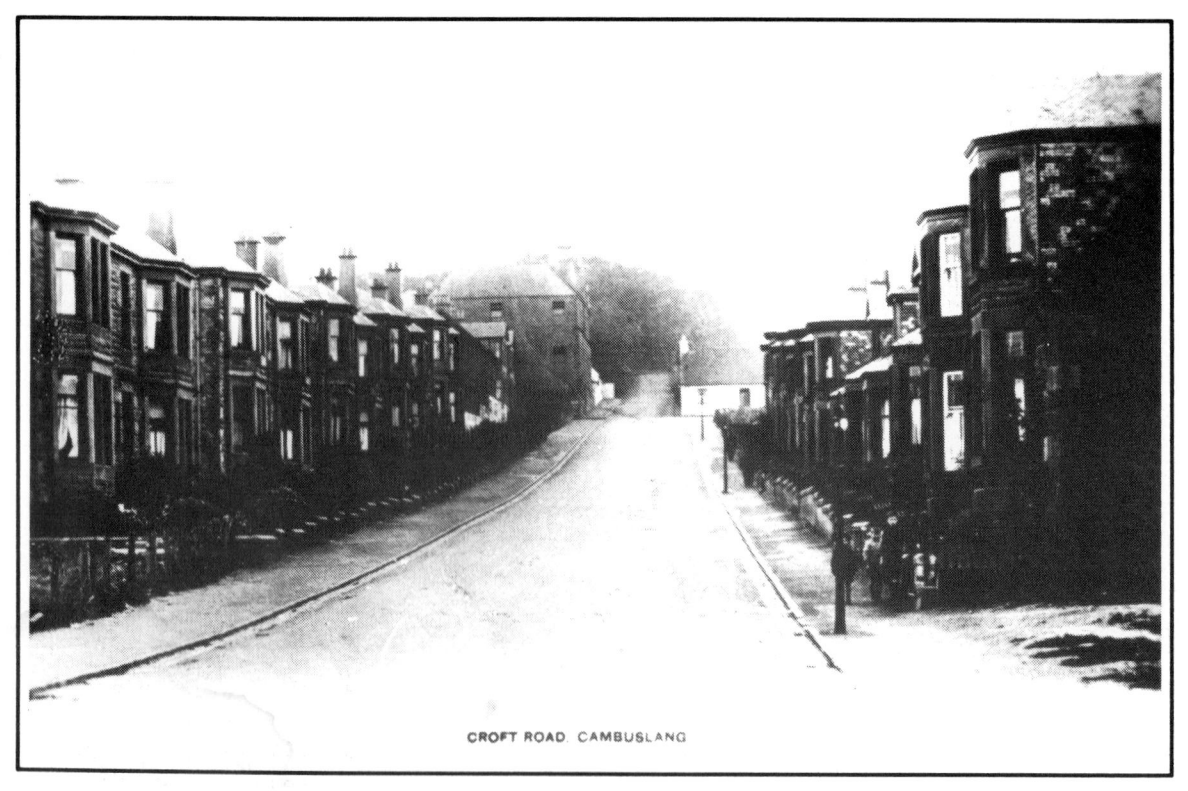

CROFT ROAD. CAMBUSLANG

46. An early scene in Croft Road at the turn of the century. On the left is Kirkhill Public School.

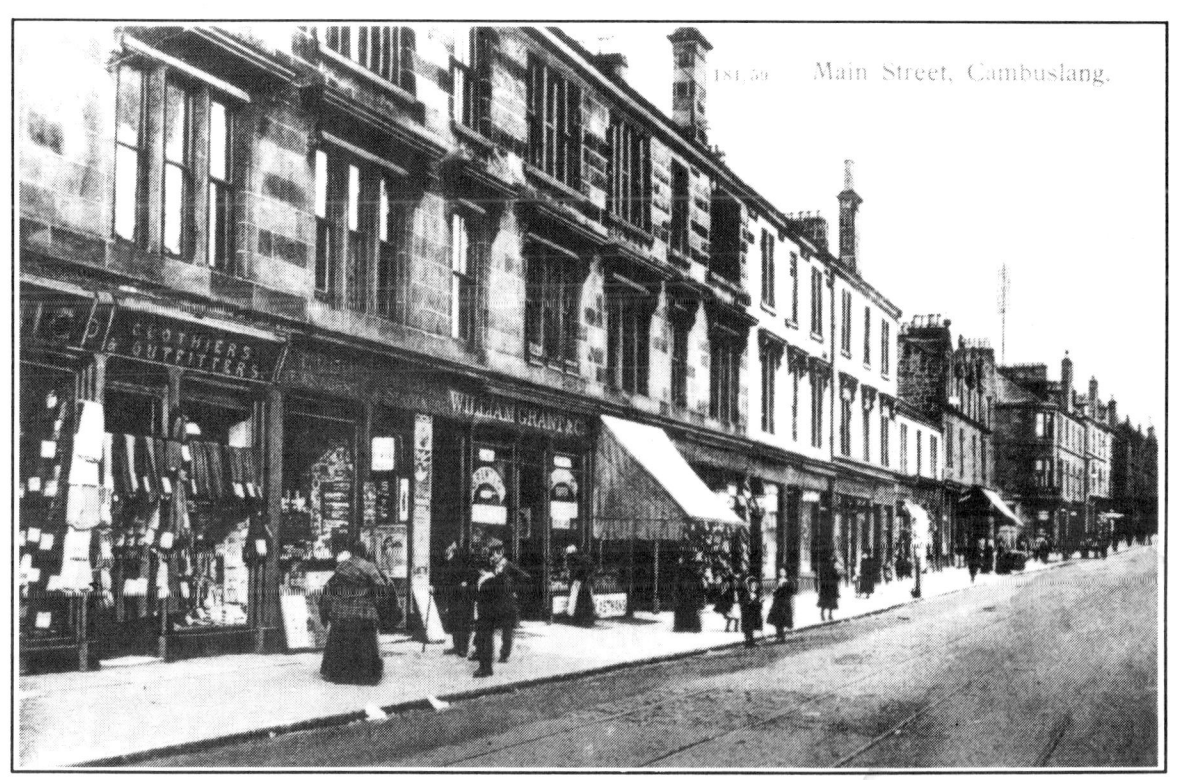

47. A busy street scene c1910.

**Further copies available
price £5.20 including UK postage from**

*Doreen Shepherd
10 Lochbrae Drive
High Burnside
Glasgow G73 5QL*